INTERIOR DESIGN FOR WELLNESS SPACES

Edited by ICI CONSULTANTS
Translated by Alison CULLIFORD

DESIGN MEDIA PUBLISHING LIMITED

©2010 by Design Media Publishing Limited
This edition published in June 2011

Design Media Publishing Limited
20/F Manulife Tower
169 Electric Rd, North Point
Hong Kong
Tel: 00852-28672587
Fax: 00852-25050411
E-mail: Kevinchoy@designmediahk.com
www.designmediahk.com

Editing: ICI Consultants
Direction: Chia-Ling Chien
Communication/Documentation: Nicolas Brizault
English Translation: Alison Culliford
Design/Layout: Chunling Yang

ISBN 978-988-19740-1-3

Printed in China

INTERIOR DESIGN FOR WELLNESS SPACES

Edited by ICI Consultants
Translated by Alison CULLIFORD

DESIGN MEDIA PUBLISHING LIMITED

CONTENTS

Spas

Beauty Institutes

Hair Salons

Spas

Designer
Andrée Putman

Anne Fontaine Spa

Twelve years after opening her first Parisian boutique, Anne Fontaine has moved into Rue Saint-Honoré, in an innovative space that brings together a boutique and a spa. The structure of the place is the result of the dialogue between Andrée Putman and Anne Fontaine, who both wanted a strong and emblematic axis to link the two spaces. Water was naturally chosen: a wall in blue Hainaut stone links the two levels, and hosts a waterfall that flows along the length of the space dedicated to the spa.

Access to the lower level is via a staircase that runs alongside the waterfall. Returning to a world that is particularly familiar to her, Andrée Putman first worked on the perspective of this long space. A mobile glass screen with an organdie fabric trapped inside it protects the privacy of the spa, but at the same time allows one to make out the spaces that compose it – up to the traditional hammam situated at the very back of the space, which offers a progression of three temperatures and a foaming bath.

The water which runs along the stone wall now moves on to the floor in the form of a small stream which leads visitors to their treatment rooms. These are arranged like a collection of asymmetrical boxes lightly suspended, in a range of off-whites: each one invites a hint of colour, such as traces of blue, green, red or violet. Their screens are in wood, impregnated beforehand with a woven canvas which leaves its traces in the heart of the material.

1. Hammam
2. Ground floor boutique

Location
Paris

Completion Date
2007

Photographer
Satoru Umetsu
Nacasa & Partners

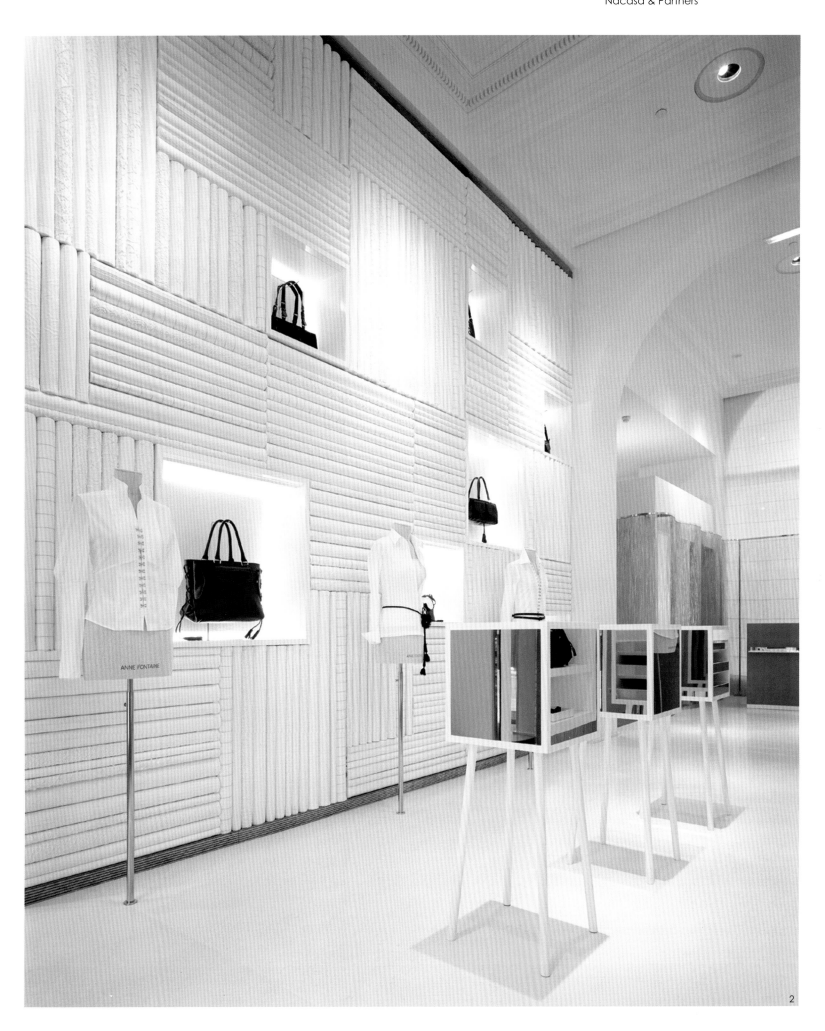

1. Staircase leading down to the spa
2-3. Entrance to the spa

1. The spa changing rooms
2. A corridor of the spa
3. Cold water plunge pool, benches in grey Corian

1. Corridor between the treatment rooms
2-5. Treatment rooms

Designer
Luc Demolombe

Aquensis

Bagnères de Bigorre and thermal waters have been closely linked since antiquity. Aquensis Spa Thermal® forms part of this continuing history. Aquensis occupies the central part of a building dating from the end of the 19th century, situated in the heart of the town. From the beginning it contained a pool fed with thermal water, becoming, in the 1950s, a centre for functional rehabilitation. It remained vacant from 1992, until the town council decided to make the most of the existing heritage and renovate this thermal building, entrusting the work to the architect Luc Demolombe.

In its design, Aquensis brings local resources to the fore, with everything centred on High Environmental Quality. Its attachment to natural materials such as wood, glass and marble is demonstrated by the spectacular choir-like roof structure in larch, which forms the main room of the Spa Thermal®. Aquensis offers the public a real dramatisation of the naturally hot and health-giving thermal waters. The natural light flows in from above, through a ceiling of glass and water situated 20 metres above the main pool and accessible to the public from the outside terraces. The presence of thermal water on the roof in winter ensures the thermal equilibrium of the whole spa, and the monumental wooden vault, which brings visual warmth and acoustic comfort, is designed to resist earth tremors. The Oriental Space gives pride of place to Pyrenean marble, which adorns the dome of the tea salon and the benches of the sequence of rooms in the hammam, which are also heated by a system that uses thermal water.

In 2010, a second phase of work gave birth to a new treatment space open to the sun terrace with a view of the Pyrenean summits. The double treatment rooms and relaxation rooms fit in perfectly with this pre-existing space, whose marble fireplaces and high ceilings testify to the golden age of this spa town.

1. View across the main pool
2. The wooden roof structure

Location
Bagnères de Bigorre

Completion Date
2010

Photographer
Dominique Julien
Pixbynot
Christian Jarno

1. Jacuzzi on the terrace in winter
2-3. The terrace with Aquaboxes
4. Relaxation room

Designer
Pascal Desprez

Spa Baumanière

Spa Baumanière is a very natural Spa with an intimate atmosphere, five hundred square meters bathed in light and tranquillity. A haven of privacy that opens onto a tree-shaded patio and a fragrant garden, the interplay of light and shadow: airy, light drapes contrasting with the dark wood of the walls and floor.

Driftwood lamps discreetly light the corridor leading to the six treatment rooms. Some are intended for body and facial treatments and beauty care; others are reserved for massages and body wraps. Thanks to its hot vapours, the hammam completely oxygenates bodily tissues and eliminates toxins. Its beneficial heat releases tensions, resulting in total relaxation. A different kind of voyage begins here, in the heart of Provence, one that leads you on the road to self discovery.

The hammam is starry, vaulted ceiling and pale walls bathe it in a peaceful light. The Sensory Pool is a voyage into a paradoxical universe, which combines the water's energy with the delicacy of the light. An aqua-sensorial experience thanks to the different massage jets: multitonic, geyser, bubbling bath... The fitness studio is equipped with all the TechnoGym cardio training essentials, including the latest version of Kinesis Personal.

1-2. The sensory pool

Location
Les Baux de Provence

Completion Date
2007

Photographer
Henk Van Cauwenbergh

1. Relaxation room with herbal tea space
2. Massage room
3-4. Corridors in the spa leading to the treatment rooms

2

3

4

1

Spa in Boscolo Exedra Nice Hotel

Situated in Nice in the new Hotel Exedra from the Italian Boscolo group, this spa is an invitation to forget it all. An underwater bubble open to the world, with an independent entrance that can welcome visitors who are not resident in the hotel, and rooted in life thanks to a symbolic tree present in the welcome area and at the heart of the swimming pool, the spa unfolds over 500m².

Modernity, the whiteness of the spaces and a filtered light, the undulations of the walls, pierced and rounded ceilings like nests of light, this architecture was dreamt up by Simone Micheli. The high point of this composition: the magnificent 15m swimming pool whose glistening mosaic creates subtle bluey reflections for a pool with the allure of a Polynesian lagoon. Waterfalls add a touch of energy to this world designed for recharging one's batteries.

Huge mirrors decorate the walls, in an environment that is soft and Zen. Six individual treatment rooms allow one to relax and a VIP room of over 30m² hosts two massage tables. A relaxation space is composed of a sauna with an integrated television, a hammam, water and ice fountain and a rest area. The fitness space is a large room with a collection of equipment dedicated to cardio-training, fitness and sport in general.

1. Reception
2. The swimming pool and its stylised waterfalls

Location
Nice

Completion Date
2008

Photographer
Hugues Lagarde

1

1. Fitness room
2. Weights area

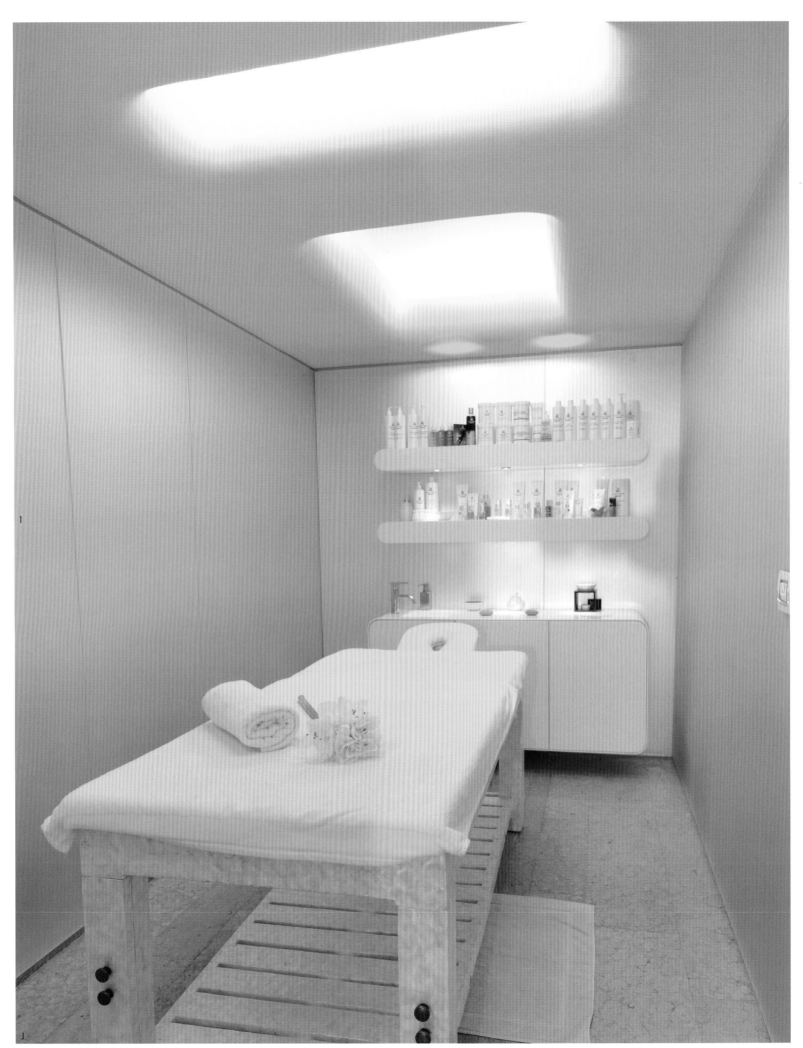

1. Bubble of light treatment room
2-3. The hammam... and its ice fountain for cooling down

1

Cinq Mondes Brussels

Fitted out in a building designed in the 1970s by the architect Stéphane Jasinski, the four-star hotel Dolce La Hulpe Brussels has dedicated 800m² to Cinq Mondes to create a prestigious spa.

A true haven of peace nestled in the heart of the forest of Soignes, the spa was designed to expand this link with the surrounding nature. To achieve this, western design has made good use of the architecture of the site, a concrete structure enveloped by glass, by placing the circulation areas and communal spaces around the edge of the spa. The reception, the corridors, the patio and the relaxation room are thus bathed in natural light and offer visitors a panoramic view of the forest. The VIP treatment room, which extends into a private terrace, also benefits from this play of interior-exterior. At the centre of the patio, an overflowing fountain emits a light, relaxing water sound without disturbing the calm in the treatment rooms. Much care has been given to the acoustics to create a place perfectly suited to relaxation and well-being.

As the hotel hosts company seminars, some spaces, like the foot and hand beauty rooms, can be combined thanks to sliding screens, thus allowing the spa to offer treatments in small groups. Stones, solid wood, textured plasterwork, the materials are noble, pure and elegant.

1. Reception and boutique
2. Drawing of the patio
3. The patio
4. Feet and hands treatment room

Location
Brussels

Completion Date
2009

Photographer
Serge Anton

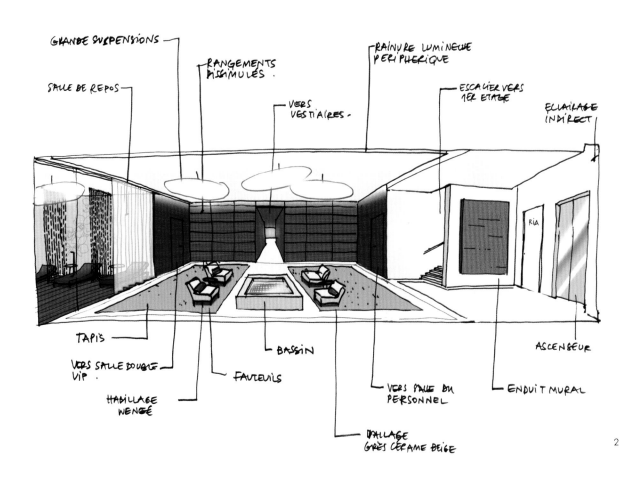

GRANDE SUSPENSIONS

RANGEMENTS DISSIMULES.

SALLE DE REPOS

VERS VESTIAIRES.

RAINURE LUMINEUE PERIPHERIQUE

ESCALIER VERS 1ER ETAGE

ECLAIRAGE INDIRECT

RIA

TAPIS

BASSIN

ASCENSEUR

VERS SALLE DOUBLE VIP.

FAUTEUILS

VERS SALLE DU PERSONNEL

ENDUIT MURAL

HABILLAGE WENGÉ

DALLAGE GRÈS CÉRAME BEIGE

2

3

4

1. Hot room in the hammam
2. Room in the hammam
3. Entrance to the spa

Cinq Mondes Paris

The first Spa of the Cinq Mondes brand was opened in 2001 a stone's throw from the Opéra, in the calm and secret quarter of Opéra Louis Jouvet Square. The colour aubergine, deep, warm and spiritual, which has become the emblematic code of the brand, is very present in the reception area of the Spa. One of the walls is covered with wenge wood against which glass shelves have been fixed to display the beauty products with magic and lightness.

The stone staircase leads to the treatment rooms. Here, connecting spaces treated in a dark colour plunge the visitor into a world of serenity. Lighting recessed into the bottom of the walls guides his or her steps and sheds dappled light like a moucharabiah. In the rooms, sliding lacquered glass screens lend a modernised Asian touch. Little by little they allow one to make out the cloakroom and the client showers, as well as the practitioners' preparation spaces.

A room with a Japanese bath, rooms called "Rain flower" or "Bliss for two" for treatments for couples, an "Aromas and Colours" hammam, each room has been designed with attention to detail to ensure the visitors' well-being.

1. Exterior facade
2. Flower rain suite

Location
Paris

Completion Date
2001

Photographer
Hervé Boutet
Christophe Maout

1. Japanese bath
2. Corridor view
3. Detail of the hammam
4. Private salon

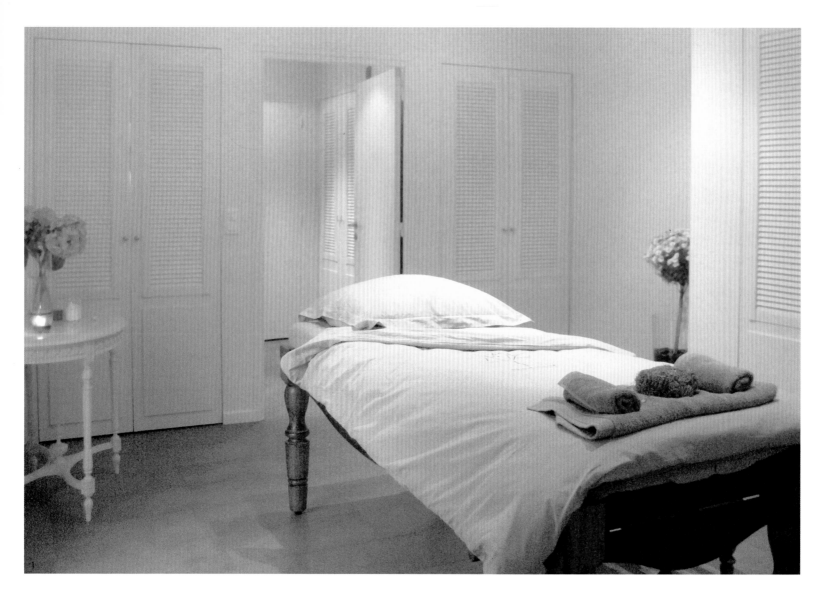

Clé des Champs

In the heart of Lyon's 6th *arrondissement*, the Clé des Champs spa offers the city's residents in search of naturalness and wellbeing a real island in which to take a breather. The interior architecture evokes the light and refined atmosphere of the French countryside as it used to be. Designed like a welcoming and convivial family home, the spa conjugates the past into the present: furniture found at flea markets has been given a new lease of life with coloured lacquer, and old prints have been used on a new scale...

Fabric-covered screens, blinds, treatment beds adorned with embroidered covers and soft pillows, warm and earthy tones woken up by a luminous and vital green, natural light coming from the planted patio, everything that you need to fully enjoy an authentic country break in the centre of the city is here.

The agency Western Design, which designed and fitted out this space, aimed to convey the world of Clé des Champs, having also developed the graphic codes for the brand's range of beauty products: a balance between authenticity and modernity.

1. Treatment rooms decorated like guest rooms
2. Antique furniture has been lacquered beige for a more modern effect

Location
Lyon

Completion Date
2008

Photographer
Western Design
Dominique Guillaudin

CLÉ DES CHAMPS
SOINS DE SAISONS

1. A relaxation room like a living room, with natural light and a view of the garden
2. Simple lines and natural materials
3. Treatment rooms decorated like guest rooms
4. A mini-boudoir for putting on make-up, decorated with wallpaper featuring an antique print reproduced to a much larger scale
5. Like a little house, the VIP room features a large shower-hammam and direct access to the garden

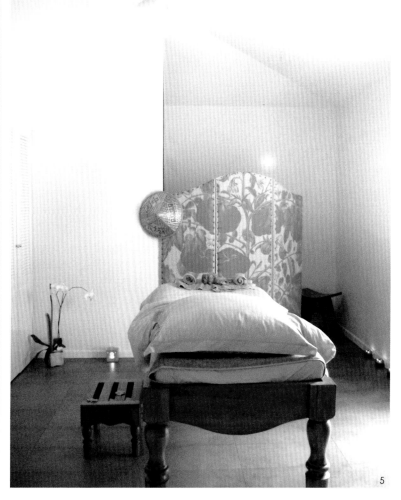

Le Clos Saint-Martin

In the heart of the Ile de Ré, the Spa of the Clos Saint-Martin is an invitation to relax, in harmony with the spirit of the isle... It offers the possibility of extending moments of lightness and serenity in a generous setting where natural stone, metal, glass mosaics and sold wood combine.

In the Spa's reception space the delicate perfume of floral essences sets the tone. At the heart of the treatment rooms a gentle tranquillity reigns: old oak floorboards that are either black or grey, matt black varnished terracotta tiles in the wet room showers. The taps, in matt nickel, bring sobriety through their lines and choice of material.

The huge hammam in hand-cut glass mosaic tiles, a celestial vault with luminotherapy and a sensory shower, featuring a rain ceiling, mists and water jets, create an atmosphere that can be as intimate as you like. In the relaxation lounge great design and the purity of the setting take precedence: natural stone from Africa, metal that is either aged or varnished matt, and natural wood. The huge volume opens out on the garden and the swimming pool and suggests comfort, luxury and fulfilment while reaping the benefits of a subtle creativity.

1. The relaxation room on the courtyard side
2. Statue by the artist Maëro

Location
Saint-Martin-de-Ré

Completion Date
2009

Photographer
Alexandra Duca

1. The relaxation room on the garden side
2. The reception area
3. View towards the relaxation room
4. The sensory shower
5. The men's dressing room

1. The hammam in glass mosaic tiles
2. The Balnéo and wrapping room

Designer
Harmonie France

Spa Comfort Zone

The Spa Comfort Zone in Paris is a real beauty lounge, nestled in the heart of the capital. Its decoration is a knowing mix of Italian and North African inspirations. The lounge or relaxation room is situated under a glass ceiling at the centre of the spa, becoming an interior patio. Its North African hammam in mosaic tiles, the presence of different exotic woods such as wenge, and a soft and filtered light, give the place a discreet luxury which comes from a contemporary interior architecture combined with treatments that sometimes date back thousands of years.

The wet part of the Spa Comfort Zone is made up of two hammam, one exclusively for women and the other for men. Each one starts with a separate room for applying savon noir or for exfoliations on the tadelakt table, different types of shower, etc., and then comes the hammam itself. This plunges visitors into a magical zone where the ceiling metamorphoses into a starry sky. This constellation with its changing colours, combined with the steam scented with eucalyptus, sends them into a gentle torpor, which the pine sauna will awaken them from.

1. View of the bar
2. Entrance and sales space

Location
Paris

Completion Date
2006

Photographer
Philippe Aouizerate

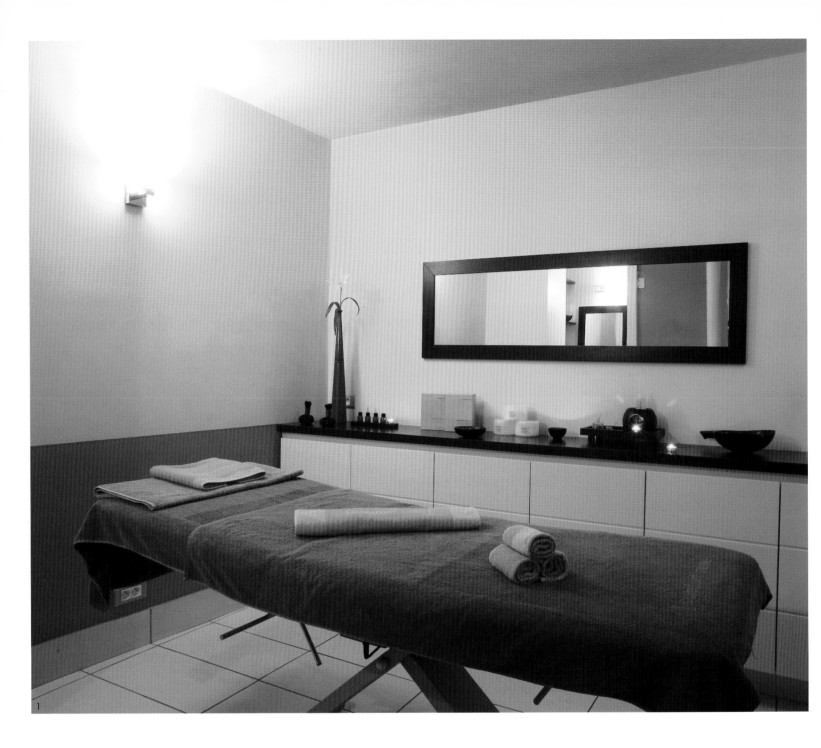

1. Single treatment room
2. Hammam

1-3. Lounge relaxation space under its glass roof

Designer
Brigitte Dumont de Chassard
Christiane Broc

Cotton'Spa

The Cotton'Spa nestles inside the Colonial Country Club Golf hotel which is situated at the heart of a clearing, on the edge of the forest of Sénart. Opened in June 2010, this 400m² luxury spa gives onto the Étiolles golf course, only 30 minutes from Paris. The space has been entirely decorated in the spirit of colonial houses by the owner of the hotel, Christiane Broc, and the spa itself fitted out by the architect Brigitte Dumont de Chassart.

This timeless place offers a relaxation pool, a swimming pool, a Jacuzzi, treatment rooms, a lounge, a bar, a hammam, an affusion shower, heated exfoliation table, VIP treatment room and a double treatment room with a private garden. Over a year of building work was necessary to bring together rare materials, superb mosaics and furniture from the four corners of the world. In each treatment room one finds paintings, sculptures and other objets d'art...

One of the musts of this spa is the Tunnel of Experiences where you can discover and rediscover unique sensations, showers at different temperatures, chromotherapy and different aromas and sounds. The spa has been awarded the quality label SPA A.

1. Reception and sales space
2. Lounge and relaxation room
3. View towards the bar

Location
Étiolles

Completion Date
2010

Photographer
Véronique Levenard

1. Double treatment room
2. Aquatic facilities: counter-current swimming, pressure-jets massage...

1. Balneotherapy
2. Hammam
3. Effusion shower

1. Cellu and Lift M6 treatment room
2. Changing rooms
3. Single treatment room
4. Double treatment room

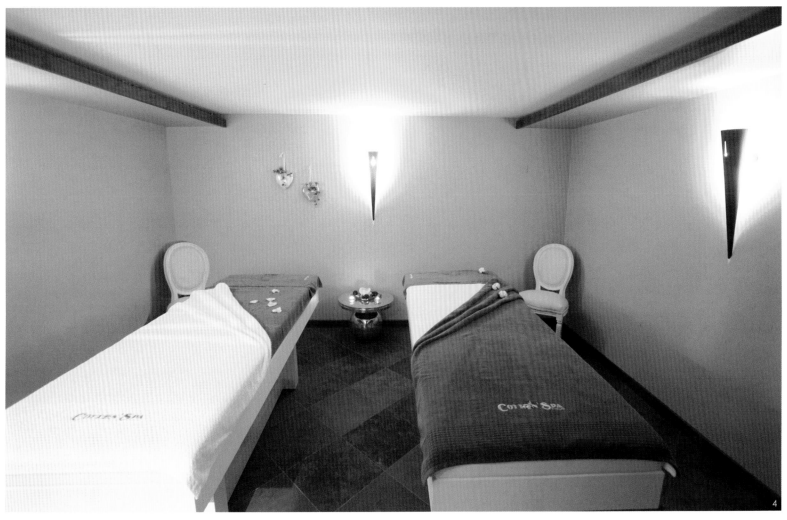

Dior Institut

In the world of haute couture there are many small rooms with big, mythical implications: models' dressing rooms, fitting rooms, VIP rooms... In the world of beauty, the mythical small room is exemplified by the treatment room, a private space secluded from the outside world where beauty care is administered to bring out the full radiance of the client's skin.

In this sense, the environment of the Dior Institut is a natural extension of the couture house, a place where the brand's emblems and signature touches are highlighted in a luxurious setting enhanced by creative lighting effects. First steps, and first impressions of the Institut: descending an historical staircase that gradually leaves the ambiance of the Hôtel Plaza Athénée behind. A wall filled with images recounts the Dior legend and opens onto a broad vaulted gallery that seems to go on forever. A central pool crowned with a glistening "droplet" of blown glass, arched arcades leading to the treatment rooms, precious materials with plush, iridescent textures...

Everything here, down to the tiniest detail, emanates incomparable luxury and refinement. All five of the spacious treatment rooms, including a double VIP room, are decorated with silver and white updated versions of Dior's emblematic medallion chairs and mirrors embellished with the "caning" motif. These symbols of the couture house are juxtaposed with the modernity of a white marble diagnosis table equipped with a state-of-the-art computer system. A relaxation and herbal tea lounge completes the Dior Institut experience, while a fitness space, hammam steam bath and sauna are available to supplement and prolong the benefits of the treatments.

1. Entrance to the Dior Institut
2. Welcome desk

Location
Paris

Completion Date
2008

Photographer
Eric Laignel
Guillaume de Laubier
Matthieu Salvaing

2

1. Plunge pool
2. Double VIP room

1. Double VIP room
2. Treatment Room
3. Emblematic Medallion Chair
4. Sauna

3

4

Designer
Jocelyne & Jean-Louis Sibuet

Les Fermes de Marie

The Fermes de Marie Spa was the first of the spas that go by the "Spa Pure Altitude" label. The pure and simple luxury of the decoration revolves around the five elements. Wood, fresh water, plants, stones and fire combine harmoniously to create a haven of serenity and contentment.

Mineral and plant ambiances come together in all the details of the spa: walls of wide planks painted grey-blue or covered with mini-pebbles, an ice fountain, swimming pool and Jacuzzi set into the large "glacier balls", these stones from the torrents of the Chamonix region rolled over the centuries by the current. The relaxation room offers to prolong the sense of softness and well-being of a "Pure Altitude" treatment. Beech, ash, limewood and birch are tangled up like in the forest or cover the walls.

The Fermes de Marie Spa is a place dedicated to the harmony of body and soul. Its 17 treatment rooms, the indoor swimming pool open onto the gardens, the outside Jacuzzi, its tea-room and its gym allow everyone to recharge their batteries after a day of skiing or simply to make the most of inimitable moments of well-being.

1. Exterior view of the spa
2. The swimming pool

Location
Megève

Completion Date
2010

Photographer
Les Fermes de Marie
DR

2

1. In the herbal tea bar
2. Entrance to the spa

1. Detail of the treatment room
2. A massage
3. Relaxation room

Les Granges d'en Haut

Opening onto the peaks of Chamonix and with an amazing view of the Mont-Blanc range, the wellness space of the Granges d'en Haut offers more than 800m² decorated in wood and stone and entirely dedicated to relaxation. This space offers you the promise of floating between the sky and the mountain peaks.

The harmony and quality of the chosen materials become the foundation of exquisite moments of relaxation. A haven of peace, the space includes five treatment rooms, including a double one with a foaming bath for massages à deux, an interior swimming pool with counter-current looking out on the Aiguille Verte, not to mention a sauna and hammam, a jacuzzi, a tropical shower and finally a herbal tea area; stone and wood are materials that are pleasant to the touch.

The treatment rooms are real cocoons of wellbeing, thanks to a pure and well conceived design. Sporty guests use the fitness studio with hi-tech equipment and enjoy a superb view of the mountains. The spa continues the spirit of the site: sober and traditional on the outside, contemporary and luminous inside.

1. The spa's panoramic terrace
2. Counter-current swimming pool

Location
Chamonix

Completion Date
2007

Photographer
Éric Cuvillier

1. Counter-current swimming pool
2. Treatment room with Japanese bath
3. A relaxation corner in the spa

1

Guerlain Spa

The Guerlain Spa opened in 2005 on the third floor of Guerlain's Parisian flagship store on the Champs-Élysées. It was a return to the source for the brand because in 1939 this same place already housed its first beauty institute. Bathed in a world of purity, whiteness and transparency, this space dedicated to facials, and body care and massages forms a luxury pause in the capital, thanks to the creativity and daring of two great talents: the interior architect Andrée Putman and the architect Maxime d'Angeac.

While the boutique on the ground floor brings together all the olfactory creations of the house, the institute opens with a hall of white marble and golden organdie kakemonos. This monumental entrance hall by Jean-Michel Frank, and the surprising alcove decorated with a Bérard tapestry, are listed, and have had to respond to the technical imperatives of the new treatments that have been developed here. Five treatment rooms have been restored with the original decor of 1939 while others mix gold and more contemporary shades of white.

Andrée Putman was an obvious choice for this project. Passionate about perfume, she slipped seamlessly into the continuity of Guerlain's history. Respectful of the artists' legacy, Andrée Putman delivers her vision of the project through the choice of materials that she is particularly fond of. Her talent appropriates light to astonish the senses. This grande dame has understood the secret of the place...

1. Perfume organ
2. Space leading to the treatment rooms

Location
Paris

Completion Date
2005

Photographer
Eric Laignel

1. Perfume organ seen from the floor below
2. Perfume fountain
3. Corridors and cosmetic spaces

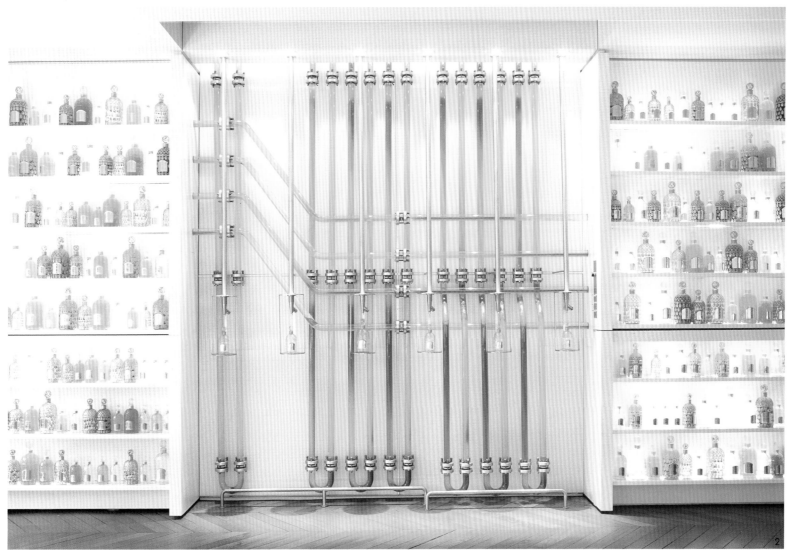

2

3

3

1. Cosmetic space
2. Pedicure space
3. Treatment room

Harnn & Thann Spa

Opened in September 2006, the Harnn & Thann spa comprises 320m² arranged around a pretty paved and tree-planted courtyard on rue Molière, between the Opéra and the Comédie Française. A recognised specialist in traditional Thai massage, the spa space has since become the emblem of the brand.

An entire wall of old pale stone and an original parquet evoke the authenticity of the place. The Spa is made up of a private hammam and five massage rooms, of which three can also host couples to share a unique moment in complete tranquillity. The time after the massage being just as important as the treatment itself, a relaxation room nesting under a glass ceiling allows one to prolong these moments of calm and serenity...

The very high ceilings, the warm colours, the subdued light of the ceiling lights and lamps in natural fibres and the Thai wooden furniture immediately give a feeling of wellbeing and comfort. The Harnn & Thann spa allows one to have a sensory experience for the body and spirit in order to combat the stress and pollution of city life.

1. Sales space
2. Staircase and relaxation room

Location
Paris

Completion Date
2006

Photographer
Frédéric Bensemhoun

1. Relaxation and foot massage space
2. Foot bathing ritual

1. Staircase
2. Shower and hammam
3. Facials and foot treatments
4. Space dedicated to massage with essential oils

Designer
Pascal Thomas (architecture)
Lisbeth Strohmenger & Karen Reichenheim (decoration)

La Clairière

The Organic Spa hotel La Clairière, a characterful place to stay, lives in total symbiosis with the lush nature that surrounds it and has a Spa that is unique of its kind: a skilful mix of the contemporary trend for minimalist design and the use of the concept of the four elements: water, earth, air and fire.

A real ode to design, this 950-square-metre world sets the tone from the beginning with an ultramodern space and pure lines which fit perfectly with the establishment's concept of holistic well-being. In this energising place flattering settings have been created giving preference to pure and structured lines. The light is soft here; glass and granite as well as muted tones, peppered here and there by a few bright touches, marry harmoniously with the warmth of wood and highlight the raw beauty of the walls in pearl grey concrete.

A few nods to faraway lands line up serenely along a water course scattered with large river stones, slender reed stems and a divine statue of Buddha, the silent guardian of the space reserved for the treatment rooms. Set into the anthracite grey stone floor, a chromatic journey invites one to move towards the relaxation space which features modern and clinical touches in beautiful settings. Elegant furniture inspired by Italian design will invite you to enjoy a fresh fruit juice in a space that opens up via large floor-to-ceiling windows onto the surrounding forest, the terrace in light wood and the stunning exterior heated swimming pool totally designed in stainless steel.

1-2. Terrace

Location
La Petite Pierre

Completion Date
2005

Photographer
Yves Trotzier
Christian Cantin

1. Spa
2. Sauna
3-4. Treatment room

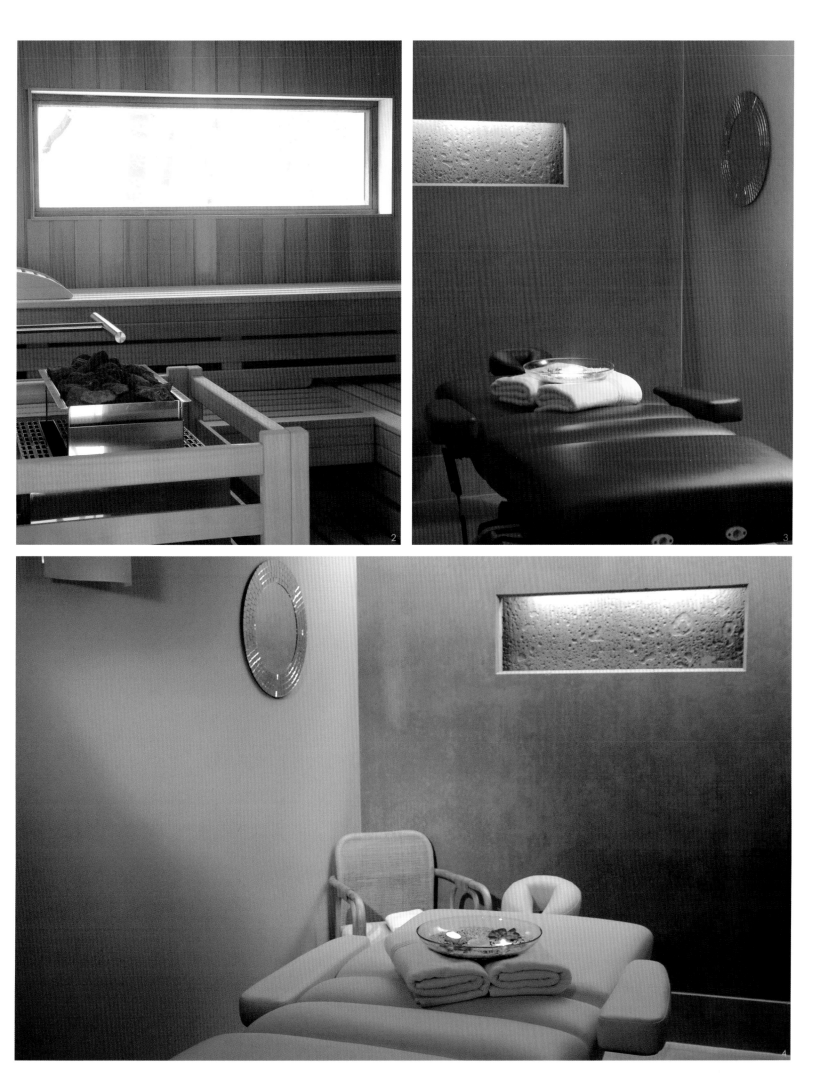

1. Silent room
2-3. Terrace

1. A relaxing ambiance
2. Cocoon leading to the exterior
3. The water

1

1-2. A serene ambiance

La Sultane de Saba

The entrance to the Spa is the display space of the La Sultane de Saba boutique, where furniture in dark wood shows the different ranges of products offered by the brand. Once past the welcome area, one discovers another world. The walls entirely covered with black pearlised mosaics are reflected in the gleam of a mirror-like floor. All the body treatments are given on three heated tables, each space possessing an ayurvedic bowl, the shirodara. Next, a hammam covered in the same black mosaic, and hosting up to six people, is an invitation to relax.

The steps towards the lower floor are dotted with candles leading to the tea salon. The pure design of the decor takes nothing away from the convivial warmth of these chairs that have come from a foreign land. A sumptuous beaded light dominates with its sparkle. The tone is given by the three massage rooms, where the chandeliers project a play of light onto the black walls. A very hushed ambiance, beyond space and time.

The first floor is reserved for beauty treatments. At the top of the stairs, a space dedicated to the pedispa, for everything to do with the beauty of hands and feet. Then come three treatment rooms, lit by daylight through high windows giving onto the majestic trees of the Cours Marigny. A black, luxurious and refined decor: ebony furniture, floor and walls in glossy and iridescent blacks, and everything lit by chandeliers with Syrian beads.

1. Superb ginger jars
2. Treatment room

Location
Paris

Completion Date
2008

Photographer
David Amsellem

2

1. The boutique
2-3. Blue hammam

1. Tea room
2. A cascade of light
3. Treatment room
4. A decorative bowl in the hammam

3

4

Designer
Jocelyne & Jean-Louis Sibuet

Lodge Park

Situated in the heart of Megève, the hotel Lodge Park is a real invitation to travel and discovery. This four star establishment, whose decoration is characterised by a trapper spirit, is only open during the winter season. Each detail has been minutely chosen with the aim of combining refinement and authenticity.

Designed in the same spirit as that of the Fermes de Marie, the Lodge Park Spa offers an environment to match that of the hotel: both very natural and very contemporary. Wood, raw granite, glass walls with rounded forms and soft colours express the five elements around which the "SPA Pure Altitude" concept revolves.

At the heart of the 500m^2 of the Lodge Park Spa, four treatment rooms with subtle colours are dedicated to relaxation and well-being. The large Jacuzzi, the hammam, the two saunas, the fitness room and the Kneipp baths allow everyone to prolong the experience. All the elements are united in this multi-sensual place to help one get back in touch with serenity and contentment.

1. The Jacuzzi
2. Kneipp bath

Location
Megève

Completion Date
2006

Photographer
Lodge Park / DR

1. Entrance and reception
2. The ice corridor

1. Treatment room interior
2. Massage room

Designer
Luc Vaichere (architecture)
Patrick Ribes (decoration)

Loreamar Thalasso Spa / Grand Hotel

In the French Basque resort of Saint-Jean-de-Luz, the classic Belle Époque Grand Hôtel increased its offer in 2007 with a magnificent thalassotherapy spa. This unique place combines a true thalassotherapy spa, led by a medically qualified team, with the luxury and beauty of a water fantasy carved into these underground vaults and opening directly onto the beach.

Designer Patrick Ribes has here made the most of the vaulted setting – a former jazz club – by dividing the 1000m² space into three lightly-stepped tiers divided by glass, so that the full area is in contact with the beach and the sea. The first area has a reception desk covered in pebbles, where guests discuss their spa programme against a background of gentle rippling from the small fountains in the ornamental pool. The marble pillars that now support the vaults were added by the designer. Below this is the relaxation area with herbal teas, which overlookeds the heated seawater pool, a green lagoon that changes colour as natural light filters through the green curtains. The raw slate wall at one end of the pool simulates a natural environment for enjoying the soothing underwater jets. At night it is covered by a starry sky. The 20 treatment rooms are either intimate cocoons or benefit from one-way glass looking out to the ocean. The fitness room – again with one-way glass – is next to a separate hammam and sauna suite. The hammam, with very low light and a starry sky ceiling, is lit by magical colours when you place your hands under the tap. This suite also includes the multi-sensory "shower experience" with its Tropical, Spring Rain, Atlantic and Polar effects. The entire spa is given ambiance by subtle uplighting, changing coloured recessed lights and candles, reflecting in the numerous mirrors and water surfaces.

1-2. The spa's reception
3. Treatment room with hydromassage bath

Location
Saint-Jean-de-Luz

Completion Date
2006

Photographer
David Bordes

1. Thai room
2. Relaxation area
3. Ayurvedic massage
4. Jacuzzi in the seawater pool

1. Star-studded pool at night
2. Shower experience
3. Heat experience

Designer
Jocelyne & Jean-Louis Sibuet

Hotel Mont-Blanc

The hotel Mont-Blanc is the legendary Megève hotel of the 1950s, whose reputation was associated with visitors such as Jean Cocteau... Jocelyne and Jean-Louis Sibuet gave back this establishment its nobility in 1994. The Spa of this jewel of Megèvian hospitality was opened in 2007. Here we rediscover all the philosophy of "Spa Pure Altitude", where the principle of the five elements is associated with a new atmosphere of purity, snow and ice.

The decoration of this "Igloo" spa gives a nod to the rooftop of Europe. From the entrance, the tangled trunks of birches mingle with walls in glacier stone to create a welcoming "Igloo" atmosphere around a chimney in lacquered white wood.

The corridor whose vaulted ceiling and walls seem powdered with snow winds around to the four treatment rooms. Each one is a subtle marriage of granite and of snowy walls to reveal the magic of this ice haven. Each detail contributes to the charm of this unique place: contemporary low lighting in the form of "snowballs" or small crystal lights at one's feet, a shower in mini-pebbles from the torrents of the region, black and white photos of plants, furniture in iron and smoked glass. The atmosphere continues thanks to the sauna, the Jacuzzi, the indoor swimming pool open to the rays of the sun and its fitness space.

1-2. Treatment room

Location
Megève

Completion Date
2007

Photographer
Hotel Mont-Blanc / DR

1. Relaxing in the herbal tea area
2. A corridor in the spa

1-3. Treatments with wintery names
4. Swimming pool
5. In the fitness room

Nuxe

In 2003 Aliza Jabès, CEO of Nuxe laboratories, entrusted Centdegrés with creating of the architectural concept of its spa. From 2003 to 2009, the Nuxe-Centdegrés partnership then gave birth to the extension of the first of the brand's spas, in rue Montorgueil in Paris, then the spa in Printemps Haussmann department store, the five star spa of the Zebra Square hotel, also in Paris, and the spa of the Hôtel Westminster in Le Touquet.

The agency started from its perception of the brand as resolutely turned towards nature, the awakening of the senses and travel, to formalise a style platform whose main theme is a tree. This Nuxe emblem structured the concept. At its origin is the earth, which gave rise to the choice of authentic, noble and natural materials (wood, stone, lava…) and warm colours (red, ivory, gold…).

Then the trunk symbolises the passage, in stages, from one state to another. It suggests an architecture made of interweavings with pathways and chambers that must be crossed to move between the different spaces, passing from one treatment to another. Finally, the crown of the tree is a metaphor for the fulfilment and feeling of elevation that the treatments bring. In accordance with the world of Nuxe, which marries effectiveness, nature and luxury, the treatment spaces preserve the intimacy of the treatment, relaxed abandon, calm, isolation (a place outside time, apart, a buffer), create an atmosphere of escape thanks to a voyage infused with ambiance and materials, and emphasise the awakening of the senses. Thanks to these spas, Nuxe positions itself as an expert brand in its domain which attracts its clients through the excellence of its products as much as through the creativity of the exclusively plant-based active ingredients used.

1. Manicure table
2. Multipurpose shower

Location
Paris

Completion Date
2003

Photographer
Nuxe

1-2. Multipurpose treatment room

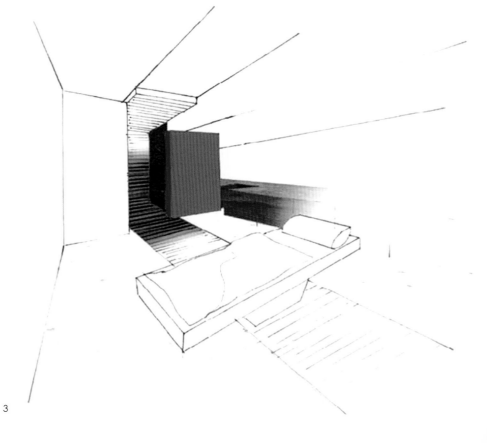

1. Double shower cubicle
2. Single shower cubicle
3. Concept sketch
4. Balneo corner

3

Six Senses Spa

The first Six Senses urban sanctuary in France has an exceptional location, a few steps from Place Vendôme and the Tuileries Garden. Six Senses, the work of the French architect Pierre David and local craftsmen, offers a Parisian interpretation of the Six Senses urban sanctuary. Admirably integrated into its environment, the place translates the beauty of the Paris sky and the Tuileries Garden with the natural and organic elements that are Six Senses' own. In the most perfect harmony, the spa unites sky, earth and natural wood.

Pierre David invited the landscape architect Patrick Blanc to create the star element of the reception space, a surprising plant wall on two levels. This luxuriant interior garden, visible from the street, offers a spectacle that exalts the senses while exercising a practical function: ridding the Paris air of pollution in order to purify that of the spa.

Another calming element in the decor, born of Pierre David's imagination: the Paris sky, projected in real time on a section of the spa wall. It allows guests to relax by becoming as one with their environment, an important component of well-being, and creates a fascinating landscape that changes with the light. The spa offers several cocoons as treatment rooms (two doubles and four singles), created in pale oak worked by hand and lined with backlit paper – evoking a Japanese lantern.

Six Senses is respectful of the environment, and its design testifies to this. The relatively small area contains no water treatment zone, which is often at the origin of waste. Situated below ground, the spa is nevertheless designed to be lit by daylight thanks to large windows giving onto the street. Everything is in high quality natural materials, pale oak and paper for the cocoon treatment rooms and furniture in oak.

1. Entrance with view of rue du Mont Thabor
2. Entrance rue de Castiglione

Location
Paris

Completion Date
2009

Photographer
Eric Laignel

1. Entrance with benches and product display
2. Plant wall and view up the staircase
3. Plant wall and staircase seen from below
4. Entrance with plant wall and shop window

1-2. Cocoon seen from behind with projection of the Paris sky
3-4. Outside of the oak cocoons

3

4

1. Treatment cocoon
2. "Reiki" session
3. Relaxation zone and oak cocoon
4. Relaxation zone

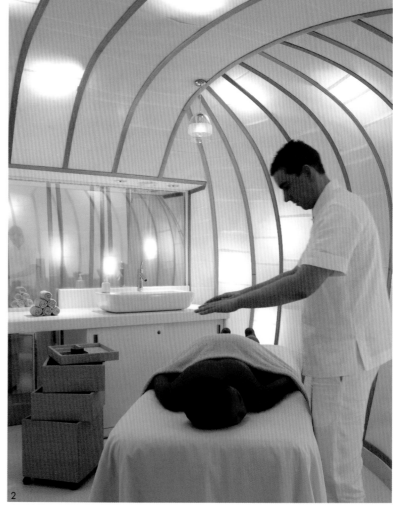

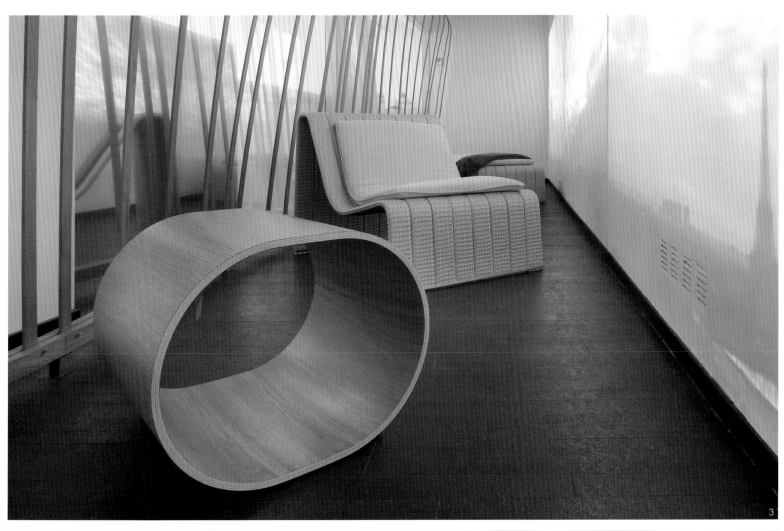

3

4

Designer
Patrick Ribes

1

Spa des Neiges / Hotel Cheval Blanc

The spa of the hotel Cheval Blanc offers a treatment space composed of four treatment rooms arranged around the reception and relaxation spaces. Patrick Ribes has designed a poetic and serene place, in harmony with the mountain, creating a setting from wood, stone and pebbles with strong contrasts: rugged and soft materials, raw wood brought together with sophisticated chandeliers, warm or subdued colours, stone walls or transparent ones...

The reception hall is panelled in wood, and through a monumental fireplace you can see the swimming pool and its rocks. A herbal tea area, situated behind, is built into walls that evoke snow. A waiting area seems to curl up in the curves of the walls. The treatment rooms are spacious and lined in pale wood and frosted mirrors which evoke winter frosts. Guests have their treatments under a starry sky provided by fibreoptics, and in indirect light that reproduces natural daylight, filtered through wooden Venetian blinds with wide slats.

The swimming pool space invites the mountain to come into the hotel and its torrents to disgorge themselves here. The bottom of the pool is covered with pebbles and flat stones. On the underwater beach, a heated rock with round and ergonomic forms provides a comfortable seat. At the back, the walls are decked out with rocks and waterfalls and the silver birch trunks are multiplied by mirrors. The beach offers comfortable day beds and a convivial fireplace area under a crystal chandelier. The sauna-hammam space is accessible from the swimming pool and offers a multi-sensory shower experience. This circular space is lined with white pebbles and lit by a blue tangential light.

1. Waiting room
2. Relaxation room

Location
Courchevel 1850

Completion Date
2008

Photographer
Thierry Malty
Marc Béranger

1. Swimming pool
2. Water bar
3. Shower experience

2

3

1

Thémaé

The design of Thémaé unfolds around the art of tea. The virtues of black, white, red and green teas are here applied to care of the body and spirit through the architecture. The interiors at Thémaé convey the essence of the cultural values of the arts of living inspired by tea.

The dominant element of the concept is found in the dialogue of dark and light tonalities of the surfaces for the abstraction of nature, and in the presence of wood for the expression of the tea ceremony. Oak, tinted pearl-grey with mat or gloss varnish, evokes the patina of time. It is used for the furniture, the flooring leading to the treatment rooms, their doors and door frames. The palette of browns evokes the faraway, hot and humid earth of the tea plantations while smooth and sometimes more luminous white breaks through here and there like clear water to refresh the ambiance instantly.

The idea of a large central table in oak, with a pure design, dominates the welcome area and gives it a convivial character. It brings together the functions of welcome, of advice, of relaxation, of tasting and sales. A suspended ceiling in oak echoes the table that it lights up, and participates in the ceremony. The ambiance becomes more hushed as one approaches the treatment room, taking the wooden path bordered with white pebbles that leads to the rooms via heavy oak doors. Each door is marked by a white light embedded in its frame. The rooms are plunged into half-light where the expression of the wood disappears and is replaced by nature: paintings and brown sandstone. Only a painted, grooved screen vibrates under the light like the rain and hides the shower and the masseurs' equipment.

1. Reception with tea tasting room
2. Corridor of the treatment zone
3. Waiting space in the treatment zone

Location
Paris

Completion Date
2007

Photographer
Marie Barlois

1. Traditional hammam
2. Traditional O'Furo Japanese bath
3. Exfoliation table

2

3

1. Private shower in each treatment room
2. Japanese teapot with flower tea
3. Traditional O'Furo Japanese bath
4. Single treatment room (for one person)
5. Double treatment room (for a couple)

4

5

Designer
Joël Robinson (architecture)
Hugues d'Achon (decoration)

Thermes Marins de Cannes

The Thermes Marins de Cannes represent French savoir faire. In this unique and modern place in Cannes, thalassotherapy has been developed in the spirit of a spa.

Indeed, the architect Joël Robinson approached the project in its context and its particularity while constantly bearing in minds the volumes and environmental concerns. The fine materials used enable the establishment to stand up to the sea water and the heat of the steam baths thanks to an aquarium in the swimming pool, aged wood which combines with the stainless steel of the staircase, and glass and waxed concrete which embellish the setting and invite the clients to relax and to regain a equilibrium between body and spirit. The decorator Hugues d'Achon has made the most of this 2700m² space, where an interesting contrast between light, water, marble, stone and glass is in evidence, allowing one to feel the luxury and calm.

Artistic creation has been explored to express light and transparency, openings and more intimate places, spaces and volumes to those who stroll about the Thermes Marins de Cannes. The walls have been built with rounded forms, creating veritable waves, just as in the corridors the pebble wall snakes like a sea serpent... On the first floor the glassmaker Bernard Pictet has designed a river of glass in the floor to represent water, the element that is omnipresent in the Thermes.

1. Indoor swimming pool
2. Outdoor swimming pool with sea view
3. Exterior terrace

Location
Cannes

Completion Date
2009

Photographer
Ralph Hutchings

1. Beauty boutique
2. Thalasso boutique and staircase
3. Waiting area
4. View of the staircase

1. Wellbeing zone
2. Exfoliation table
3. River of glass representing the sea
4. Shower experience
5. Caldarium

1. Relaxation room
2. Treatment room with hydromassage bath
3. Beauty treatment room
4. Double treatment room for seaweed wraps

3

4

Designer
Jean-Philippe Nuel

Ultimate Spa/Château de Villiers-le-Mahieu

In the setting of listed 13th-century château, the spa is a complete project encompassing architecture and decoration. The ambition was to integrate it into the site while asserting a modernity that excludes any form of pastiche. In its topology, the architecture uses the archetype of rural constructions: a long building with a 45° roof slope, but also natural materials like wood and stone, which contrast with the modernity of glass.

In the interior, the spa plays with the horizontality of the ground floor, the floor and the ceiling answering each other in the same black tonality. This mirror effect extends to the swimming pool which echoes a glass ceiling. Thus composed, the space opens up and closes in three dimensions. The colour purple creates a dialogue with the black; this colour is the expression of nature and also figures in the project in the close-up flower photographs by Gilles Trillard. The rooms illustrate this rurality through the use of the same chromatic range, through their sobriety and the use of materials such as the straw used to make the bedheads.

1. Exterior view of Ultimate Spa
2. Massage room with mood enhancers: light, U.V, music, etc.

Location
Villiers-le-Mahieu

Completion Date
2007

Photographer
Christophe Bielsa

1. The pool is enlivened by massage jets, a counter-current, massage, and echoes the placing of the skylights
2. Massage room which plays of the fluidity of the space while privatising the individual cells
3. Fitness room

2

3

Designer
Pascal Desprez

U Spa Barrière

In the new wing of the hotel Majestic Barrière, U Spa Barrière unfolds over 450m². Like the rest of the extension of the Cannes palace hotel, its decor was designed by the interior architect Pascal Desprez. He has created a sophisticated ambiance, made up of contrasts and elegance.

The spa contrasts white marbles with precious woods, and the minimalistic aesthetic of the equipment with the warm comfort of large benches and cushions. As soon as they arrive, clients feel as if they are in an elegant cocoon, a first step towards wellbeing and a beautiful introduction to the pleasures distilled in this place. U Spa Barrière encompasses, among others, four treatment rooms, including a double equipped with a Balnéo bath for moments of relaxation shared between friends or as a couple. It has made its mark as one of the principle references for "wellness" on the Côte d'Azur and also offers a sauna, a hammam, a relaxation room, a fitness room and, exclusively on the Croisette, the "Water Paradise" room.

At the base of this original concept is a fun variation on showers. But by playing with olfactory, sonic and luminous ambiances to stimulate the senses and the imagination, by changing the temperature and force of the water several times, it transforms a simple shower cabin into a real multi-sensory journey. With four successive ambiances – Cold breeze (blue and white lights, cold water and fresh mint aromas), Summer storm (red and white lights, 39° water), Cold rain (green and white lights, cold water) and, to finish, Tropical rain (amber lights, 39° water, passion fruit aromas) – the Water Paradise experience sends the user into a rare moment of relaxation and escape.

1. Herbal tea room
2. Sauna
3. Double treatment room

Location
Cannes

Completion Date
2010

Photographer
Studio Harcourt Paris
Éric Cuvillier

1. Hammam
2. Double treatment room

1

2

Villa Thalgo

Refined, intimate and convivial at the same time, everything in this space has been dreamed up, considered and studied in order to offer a pause of absolute relaxation. The setting on Place du Trocadéro, the choice of materials (a marriage of stone and different types of wood), the layout of the place, everything is simple, precious and warm.

Thalgo decided to weigh anchor for its new Spa at garden level, a few steps from the Maritime Museum, Museum of Mankind and Great Aquarium of Paris. A swimming pool, hammam, spacious treatment rooms... the architects worked for months to devise a real "marine showcase" of more than 800m² which transports visitors into a sea ambiance. As soon as one enters, the calming and reviving voyage begins, with water as its guiding line.

Symbolised by three spaces that follow on from each other and complement each other, the Spa Villa Thalgo offers a three-part journey: the tonic space, with the fitness room and aquagym, the unwinding space around the pool, the lounge and the terrace, the treatment and relaxation space with its hammam, its treatment rooms and relaxation room.

The Square of Sensations, with its seven treatment rooms, offers spaces entirely dedicated to well-being and beauty where the attention to detail sets the tone of the house: on the walls, drawings of seaweed in copper leaf recall the world of the sea. Last but not least is the VIP treatment room, which is particularly spacious and comfortable. Designed in the spirit of a "private Spa", it is decorated in an ochre colour and has its own wet zone in slate and black pebbles.

1. Entrance of the Spa Villa Thalgo
2. Circulation space
3. Pool with hydro-massage
4. Large seawater hammam

Location
Paris

Completion Date
2009

Photographer
Thomas Dhellemmes,
Atelier mai 98

1. Double treatment room
2. Treatment room

Wellness Beauty

Wellness Beauty Natural Spa is a showcase dedicated to top of the range services, removed from decorative excesses. Its concept rests on highly defined axes, envisaged as the two sides of a leaf. A discreet and efficient functionality, ethically responsible through the use of a form of low-energy lighting (powerful LEDs, fibreoptics), ecological water management and treatment, and ergonomic furniture composed of natural materials selected according to environmentally responsible criteria. A dreamlike space, a door opening on a sensory journey outside time. Two spaces on two levels, one a sober but welcoming reception area, the second a crypt dedicated to the sensory.

From this perspective the choice of discreetly luxurious materials takes into account the harmony of the five types of energy – wood, fire, earth, metal and water – which led to the largescale use of microbeaded light wood veneer for the relaxation space, revealing its soft texture. Stone floor tiles, and glass and bamboo mosaics decorate the spacious treatment rooms which are each considered as a world in itself.

Particular attention has been paid to the ceilings to offer an invitation to let go and promote relaxation. The lighting, an essential component for creating a magical impression, was envisaged as a fundamental material, a subtle support for the treatments given.

As the apogee, the floor of the relaxation space was envisaged as a vast plate of patinated bronze made from resins and powdered bronze, copper, brass and gold. Its surface is an invitation to explore that is both tactile and visual with the silent progression of 400 glistening fibreoptics points which deliver a slow, otherworldly movement while imperceptibly guiding the gaze towards each door. The general spirit of the place is in fact the vector giving life to the archetypal value of the Moment. A certain sacredness gives it life and sends it out invigorated, calmed, gives it its reason for being.

1. The relaxation lounge with its floor illuminated with stars
2. Massage room with gold leaf decoration and Indian stone

Location
Lyon

Completion Date
2008

Photographer
Philippe Ferrer

1. The reception area, presenting the different textures and aromas of the treatments
2. Cleopatra Balneo with rose petals

1. Mosaic hammam, eucalyptus scents and a magical wall of streaming water
2. Ladies' changing room with a unique sink in the form of a watch bracelet
3. Affusion shower offering a divine rain massage

Spark
斯巴尔克水疗馆

In October 2006 Les Rives Lucien Barrière opened Spark, Beauty, Sport & Spa, a sensory world of wellbeing, which was followed in January 2011 by Médi-Spark, a new concept devoted to medical and beauty treatments. Spark offers a unique concept that brings together beauty, sport and a spa in a magnificent setting. Facing the lake, Spark has been decorated by Pascal Desprez, who has created a serene and harmonious space marrying wenge wood and white stone. Behind the large picture windows, the sun floods this new 3500m^2 space.

As soon as one enters, the bath robes are like an entry card for penetrating this world of original purity. Two luxury hotels, renovated by the decorator Jacques Garcia, frame the new building. Their translucent footbridges allow clients to go directly to Spark from their rooms in their bath robes. To lounge in the Reviving Waters, revitalise your skin with the World Exfoliations, awaken your senses enjoying the Sensational Massages, take care of yourself with the Sparkling treatments or rediscover a Hint of the East with the traditional benefits of the hammam... The

treatment rooms and massages are at the heart of this relaxation space, with two "couple rooms" made up of two massage tables, a double tub and double shower. Each of them has its own terrace.

Over 250m^2, the "midair" FitSpark space has sophisticated, high-performance equipment for fitness, muscle-building and cardio-training incorporating hi-tech systems for personalised programmes and virtual coaching. In a harmonious and invigorating space, Spark offers its clientele the sine que ultra of aquatic relaxation with the "Opale Onsen", two saunas and two Oriental hammams with their traditional treatments. The south-facing, private, overflowing swimming pool has the unique dimensions of 18m by 7.5m.

1. The Opale Onsen space and the counter-current pool
2. Relaxation space beside the swimming pool

Location
Enghien-les-Bains

Completion Date
2006

Photographer
Stéphane Morsli
Jean-Marc Tingaud

1. Swimming pool
2. Opale Onsen pool
3. Swan's neck and geysers in the Opale Onsen pool

2

3

2

3

1-2. Central atrium
3. Relaxation room
4. Spark's main staircase
5. Reception area

4

5

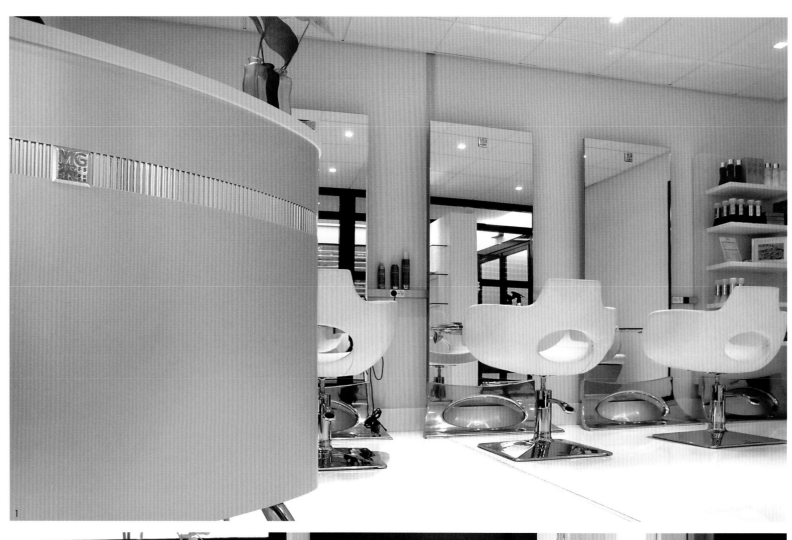

3

1-2. Spark hair salon
3. Women's relaxation room
4. Hammam

4

1&3. Double treatment room
2. Double treatment room with lake view
4. Treatment room with Japanese bath

3

4

Beauty
Institutes

du bout des doigts.

Audebert Institute

The clientele was loyal... but the owner wanted to give the place a new appeal through a complete overhaul! The sales space on the ground floor has been enlarged and livened up with a manicure space. The distribution of the different spaces gives a general feeling of balance which eliminates the impression of narrowness and makes circulation as easy as possible. Modular presentation units show off the products. The lighting allows one to vary the intensity of light according to the time of day. The contrasts created between light and shade give the whole place a new dynamism.

The treatment rooms have been given a new look using a more ergonomic, more modern material and a relaxing orangey light for more comfort. Smooth materials like Corian, intimate colours, pale pink, Parma violet, purple, contribute to this atmosphere of relaxation and wellbeing while giving a note of freshness and lightness.

The visual coherence between the logo, the light graphic treatment of the walls, the leaflets and bags creates a unity and a complicity with clients, from the exterior (the façade) to the interior, while adding a sophisticated and feminine note.

1. Treatment and product spaces that cohabit harmoniously
2. Poetic graphics express the spirit of the place and punctuate the succession of spaces

Location
Paris

Completion Date
2005

Photographer
Henri Perrot

1. An attractive product display leads to clarity of the offer
2. Ground floor plan
3. A colourful and lightly graphic wall leads the client in
4. Wall graphics to welcome and orient the clients

2

3

4

1. A pure design in a contemporary style
2. Simplicity of lines and colours to create a soft and feminine ambiance
3. Below ground plan
4. Optimal comfort in a chic and relaxed ambiance
5. Back lighting has been used to create a soft and cosy atmosphere

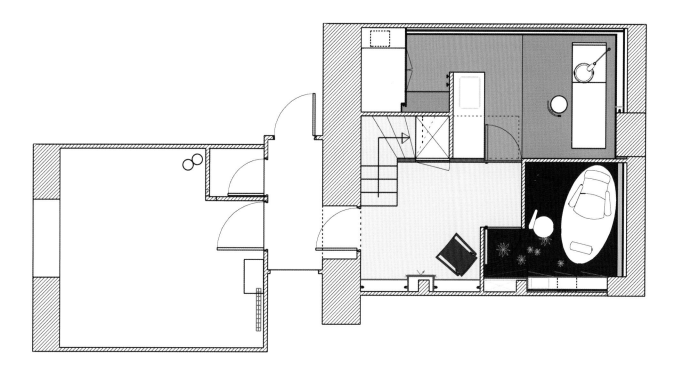

3

4

5

Designer
Frédéric Gaunet

Biologique Recherche

In the heart of Paris, on the Avenue des Champs-Élysées, in the calm of the courtyard of an old hôtel particulier, Biologique Recherche has had its pilot institute, l'Ambassade de la Beauté (the beauty embassy) since 1993. With its welcoming ambiance, its hushed intimacy and its technical surfaces, everything is dedicated to holistic beauty.

The choice of noble materials is deliberate and echoes the richness of the Biologique Recherche preparations, which are heavily endowed with pure active ingredients. The design and the furniture were created to order by cabinet makers and artist glassmakers in the blue, white and gold colours of the brand. Everything revolves around the skin, its texture, its softness, and also its rhythm. Everywhere you rest your gaze there are curves: an ode to respect and to softness.

On one side, luxurious materials, pleated silks, gold leaf engraved and applied by hand on mirrors furrowed into regular waves; on the other technical surfaces in Corian and mobile, ergonomic seats. In the entrance hall, two rugs that are deep both in colour and quality recall two beans forming a cell. The armchairs, like protective hulls in silk velvet, offer a second skin. The desks are in raw oak varnished mat for lastingness. The metallic pieces, handles and bases, are in nickel for its raw and technological look, microbeaded for softness to the touch. In the treatment rooms, ruffles of gold around the light bulbs make the lighting intimate and warmer, the seats are in white leather and the preparation surfaces are in Corian.

Frédéric Gaunet gave l'Ambassade de la Beauté its new face, succeeding in reconciling warmth, softness and intimacy for a personal welcome with the more technical needs demanded by the Biologique Recherche methodology.

1. On the ground floor, away from the hustle and bustle of the Champs-Élysées, the warmth of the reception with white and deep blue the dominant colours
2. Everywhere one looks there are curves: an ode to respect and softness

Location
Paris

Completion Date
2008

Photographer
Jean-François Gaté

1. Sober lines of the welcome desk
2. A simple and serene treatment room

1. Softness and intimacy of the double treatment room
2. Purity, authenticity and nobility of materials
3. The refinement and delicacy of the decor make one feel at home
4. An armchair in silk velvet like a protective cocoon

Designer
Centdegrés

Carita House of Beauty

In 2008 Centdegrés designed the architectural concept for Carita House of Beauty in Paris, as part of an approach to the global vision of the brand, integrating the overhaul of the visual identity as well as the packaging of the Haute Beauté Corps et Cheveux line. The legendary address, 11 rue du Faubourg Saint-Honoré, is directly connected to the visionary spirit of the Carita sisters. For more than fifty years it has welcomed women of all ages who have complete confidence in the knowledge and expertise of these "beauty craftsmen". In calling on Centdegrés, Carita wanted to strengthen the link with its origins and to reawaken in this place the spirit of luxury and prestige that has made this brand a reference in Global Beauty.

Conceived as a showcase for the brand, the space is designed like a reassuring cocoon for women, which lends itself to the game of metamorphosis.

The pure and voluptuous lines of modern furniture design fit harmoniously into the Haussmannian inner sanctum where Parisian chic manifests itself in a central majestic staircase. Lighting is at the centre of the concept. It is omnipresent and optimised by the play of frosted mirrors, an alternance of shiny and matt wall lacquers and the introduction of an unusual lilac tint which makes the white and black of the original code resonate.

The soul of the brand has been reintroduced in this emblematic house and now the Carita sisters, whose portrait once again graces the walls, watch over it... In 2009, Centdegrés won a Gold Award at the Popai European Awards for the best creations of the year in POS, digital media, commercial architecture and interior design for the architectural concept for Carita.

1. Entrance to the House of Beauty
2. Salon and waiting space
3. Hair advice and diagnosis space

1

Location
Paris

Completion Date
2008

Photographer
Carita

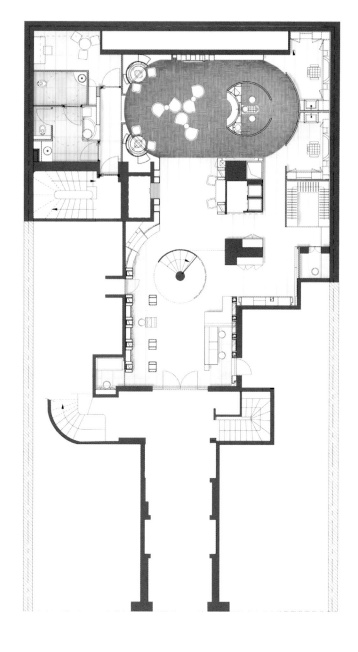

1. Front door
2. Installation plan
3. Entrance hall

3

1. Display tables
2. Close-up of a display table
3. Carita sisters sample bar
4. Display wall leading to the cloakroom

3

4

Designer
Sylvie Zerat

Carlota Institute

In Paris's 8th *arrondissement*, on prestigious Avenue Hoche, the Institut Carlota prides itself on its celebrity clients and the quality of its treatments. A specialist in the finest manicures and pedicures, it also offers facials and body care using the exclusive Carlota products that are based on natural ingredients and North African savoir-faire (orange flower, honey, musk, savon noir and exfoliation salts). The whole place was redecorated in 2009 injecting the freshness of mauve, fuschia and blue.

The entrance is pure white, with the Carlota silhouettes enlivening the space between door and window, printed on the wall in black and fuschia. Smart brushed steel and slate-coloured walls enter for the reception desk, backed by an aquarium framed in steel, and with mauve bottled products giving a taste of what is to come.

These three themes of mauve, white and steel characterise the manicure area which is both convivial and intimate, with its individual manicure desks and mauve shelves showcasing the products. The floor is in a warm stone, and soft spotlights arranged randomly in the ceiling complement the focused table lamps.

Next follows a chromatic journey: the three treatment rooms with their mauve, blue and fuschia decor combined with white, a relaxing suffusion of colour where even the towels are dyed to match perfectly the painted walls and discreet cupboards. Central to Carlota's beauty approach is the hammam, and this too has been newly redecorated with beautiful stone tiles and a starry night effect. It is marvellously relaxing and softens the skin as the perfect preparation for Carlota's exfoliation and massages.

1. Reception
2-3. View of the manicure spaces

Location
Paris

Completion Date
2009

Photographer
Thierry Begin

1. Hammam
2. Exfoliation room

1. Mauve treatment room
2. Dome treatment room
3. Blue treatment room
4. Pink treatment room

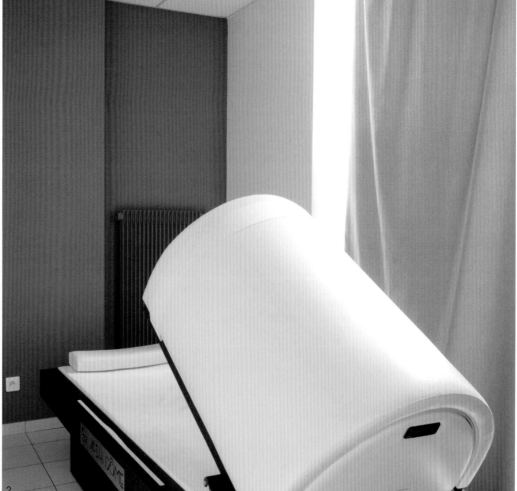

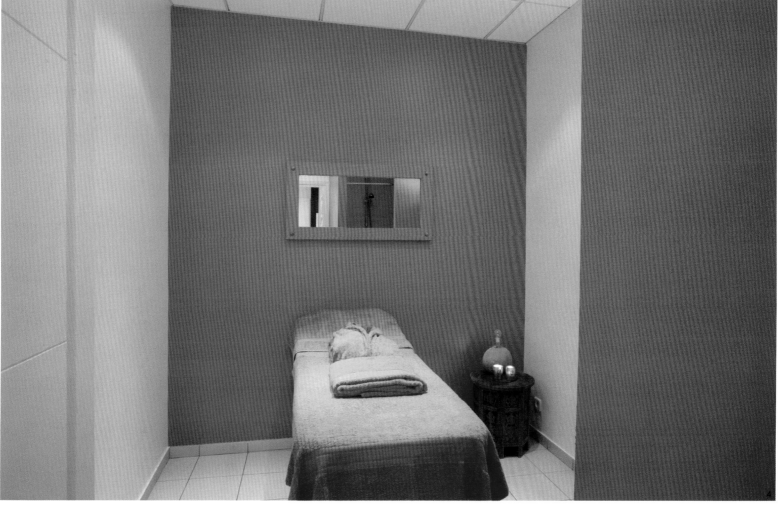

Diva Institute

A place of welcome, sales and treatments, the space laid out had to organise the institute and hierarchise its functions. A single, unique piece of furniture that runs all around the periphery fulfils this function. Soft and curved in a rectangular space, the piece twists and turns, first guiding the eye and then the visitors themselves. Panels of translucent glass protect one from prying glances from the street. Shelves freely encircle the walls, surrounding colours and mirrors.

The brief was to be light, creating a white and pink beauty institute. The response was obvious: white for the furniture and the shelves, a patchwork of pinks for the floor, the walls and the jewellery display panels. The design uses and reinterprets all the existing elements: the two columns are used to great effect and mark the entrance to the treatment rooms, the fuse box is covered in pink fabric, attention has been paid to the ceiling lights, etc. Diverse impressions and sensations mix and mingle.

The furniture has pure and smooth lines, the flooring is soft and comfortable, the columns spiked with coat hooks, and the vertical display cases are in fabric overlaid on soft foam. The light sources are direct and indirect and the shelves and furniture dress up and give meaning to the place.

1. The fittings give a sense of flow to the space
2. Soft, comfortable and colourful flooring

Location
Ploudalmézeau

Completion Date
2009

Photographer
Eno Architectes

1. Mirror integrated into the wall shelving
2. Counter integrated into the main furniture block
3. Mirror integrated into the wall shelving
4. Make-up table

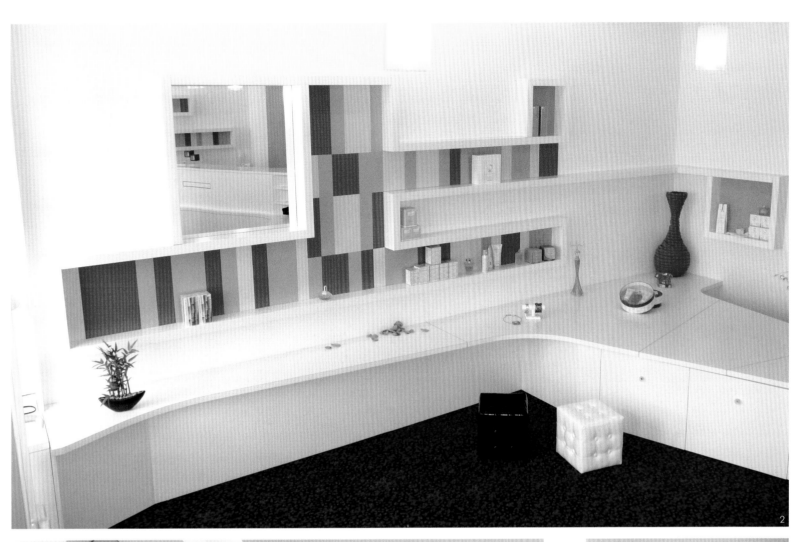

2

3

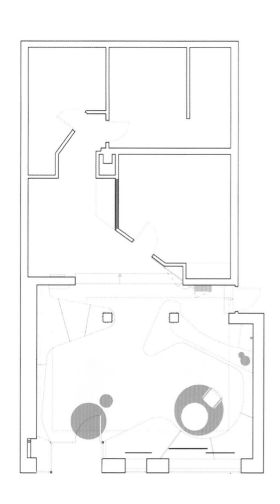

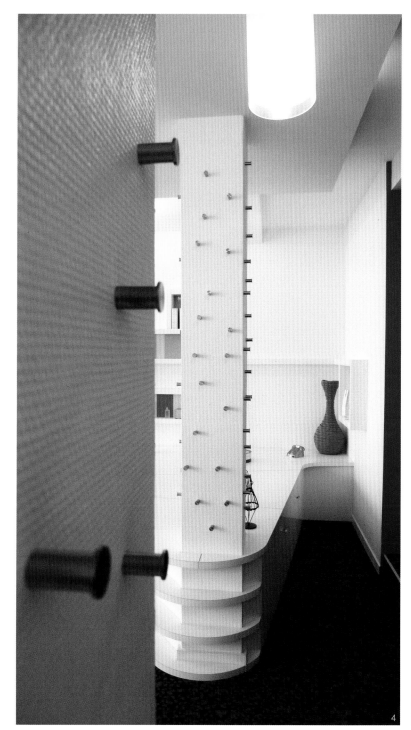

1. View from the treatment rooms situated at the back
2. Shelving curving round the entrance wall
3. Plan
4. Columns bristle with coat hooks
5. Good lighting makes the most of what was already there

1

L'Espace Weleda

"To create a place conducive to serenity where human beings are brought to rediscover their place in the natural world…" This was the project undertaken by Maryam Ashford-Brown, architect of the Espace Weleda: an attempt to establish a delicate balance between the spiritual and the material.

And the gamble paid off! The materials were selected as much for their own characteristics as for their symbolic implications, with constant attention paid to respect for the environment: granite, oak, natural stones, wood from local tree species, ecological paint… three hundred square metres of well-being under the sign of naturalness but also of modernity is thus offered to the public. On two levels with a mezzanine, the Espace Weleda, with its deep and large spaces, instils a real feeling of liberty, of calm, of tranquillity, of regeneration and of comfort.

All the elements of the decor were designed by Maryam Ashford-Brown in collaboration with artists chosen for their own talents: Yann Grégoire for his sculptures in stones, Japanese designer Shu Moriyama for her screenprints on glass, Greek artist Lanna Andréadis for her transparent outlines of plants, graphic designer Jacqueline Brétar for the typography elements in the decor. Other artists will intervene from time to time so that this place is never exactly the same, and will be like a vital breath charged with permanently renewing energy.

And the famous botanist Patrick Blanc has created a plant wall standing at the entrance to the Space like a breath of vitality. It testifies to the medicinal virtues of the plant world. Completely naturally, the presence of the plants purifies the air and creates a break with the polluting activity on the outside.

1. Panoramic view of reception area
2. Plan of ground floor
3. Reception desk

Location
Paris

Completion Date
2006

Photographer
Jean-Michel Labat & Philippe Caron

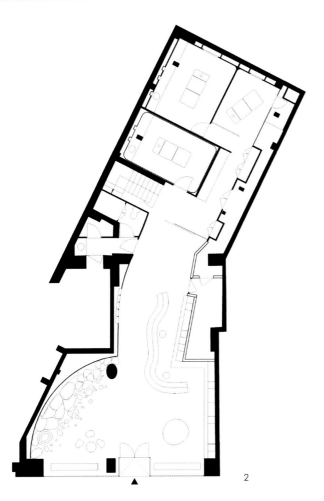

2

3

1. Glass façade on the Avenue Franklin-Roosevelt
2. Standing Stone and Stone Bowl designed by M.A-B and
   sculpted by Yann Grégoire

1. Vertical Garden by Patrick Blanc
2&4. Reception area
3. Exhibition area leading to massage parlours

3

4

1. Reception desk designed by M.A-B
2. Upper floor plan
3. View from balcony
4. Music room

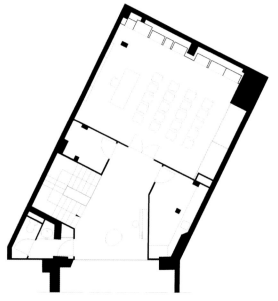

2

3

4

1. Meeting room
2. Detail of stairway
3-4. Massage parlours

3

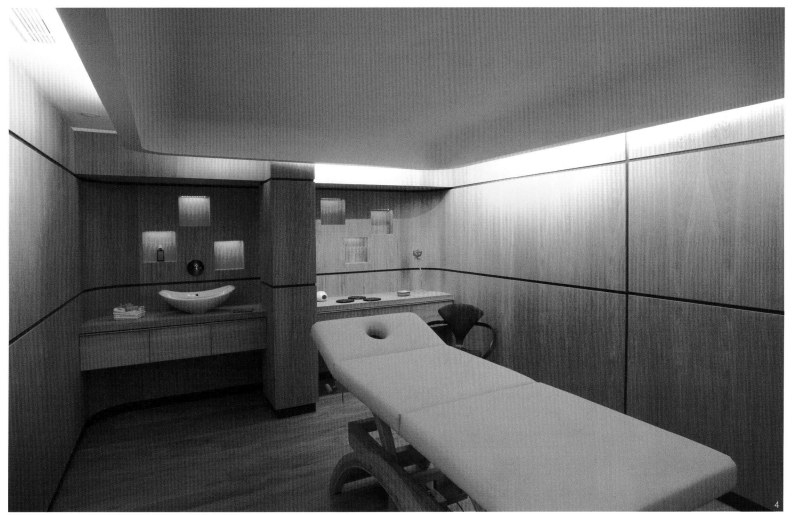

4

Designer
Thierry Lombardi

Jean-Claude Biguine – Prado Avenue

Though it is not evident when you see it today, the first particularly of this project resides in the original configuration of the commercial space. The main room giving onto the cinema Le Prado resembled a kind of cube that was badly laid out and directionless. A square plan, high ceilings and no work done on the lighting. It was a volume in which everything floated, listless and shapeless.

In order to give it back the sense of energy that comes from elongated proportions, this volume has been split in two along its length, which also restores the logic of the great ceiling height. To make the space even more dynamic, the lateral right field has been distorted by putting in place three inflections. Meanwhile the lateral left field is made up of a single movement, a single line of 13 metres in the heart of which are implanted the eight hairstyling stations. With the volume starting to elongate, we start to feel the effects of this kind of very structured canyon, with angular or stretched out forms.

Next comes a veritable work of sculpture in three dimensions, with the aim of strengthening, of accentuating the different volumes, inflections and feeling of infinite stretching out of the lateral left wall: a suspended false ceiling and coloured back lighting, a single mirror 14 metres long, also backlit and incorporating four LDC screens, luminous shelves and a monolithic cash desk in immaculate white. For ambiance, the lower level finds its equilibrium in surroundings inspired by the polar circles: a virginal white (white walls, white lacquered furniture, white sinks and shampooing chairs in white imitation leather), mirrors and raw steel, blueish frosted glass, chrome taps, crystal chandeliers... The ceiling is the only element that announces the ambiance of the floor above: baroque elegance and medieval mystique through the powerful alchemy of black and gold. Black for the walls, black for the floor, black for the ceilings, black for the doors, black for the furniture, the electrical fittings, the spotlights, the air-conditioning outlets, the light switches. A total blackout electrified by the thousand flames of gold elements: furniture, door handles, hanging chains and the hammam.

1. Access to the spa
2. Hair styling space

Location
Marseille

Completion Date
2007

Photographer
Pierre Ciot

1. Subdued ambiance
2. View from the entrance

1. Hair styling station
2. Plan of the ground floor
3. Plan of the first floor
4. Relaxation space in the spa

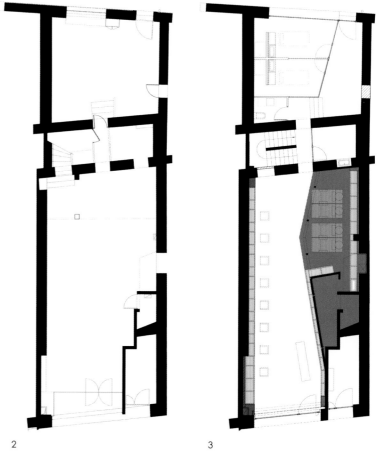

2

3

4

Designer
DC&R / Catherine Diot-Clément & Florence Renouf

La Colline Institute

The La Colline treatment space has been totally revisited to become the Parisian signature of the brand. In this exclusive beauty treatment space, the founding principles of La Colline are brought together to offer a Swiss cocoon of serenity and technical prowess.

The white slightly tinged with sky blue of the glaciers envelops the institute. The play of translucent materials brings luxury, sobriety and refinement to the place. A truly relaxing pause between the outside and inside worlds, the waiting area is specially designed to invite the body and spirit to enter into a moment of peace. The red of this cocoon marries with the luminous purity of white in an essentially Swiss combination. White crosses in relief slip soberly into the decor and guide one naturally towards the treatment rooms. At the foot of the stairs, a few steps announce the space allocated to beauty treatments, divided into four cabins that are as comfortable as they are practical.

Stone, water and air meet in this contemporary institute: drops of oxygen are suspended in the ceiling lights, and flow along the mineral walls, reflecting the cellular oxygenation brought by the CMA® complex of active ingredients that is at the heart of the La Colline products. Molecules and cells lend their rounded design to the decor and become elements in the furniture.

1-2. Reception space

Location
Paris

Completion Date
2009

Photographer
Paul-Olivier Doury

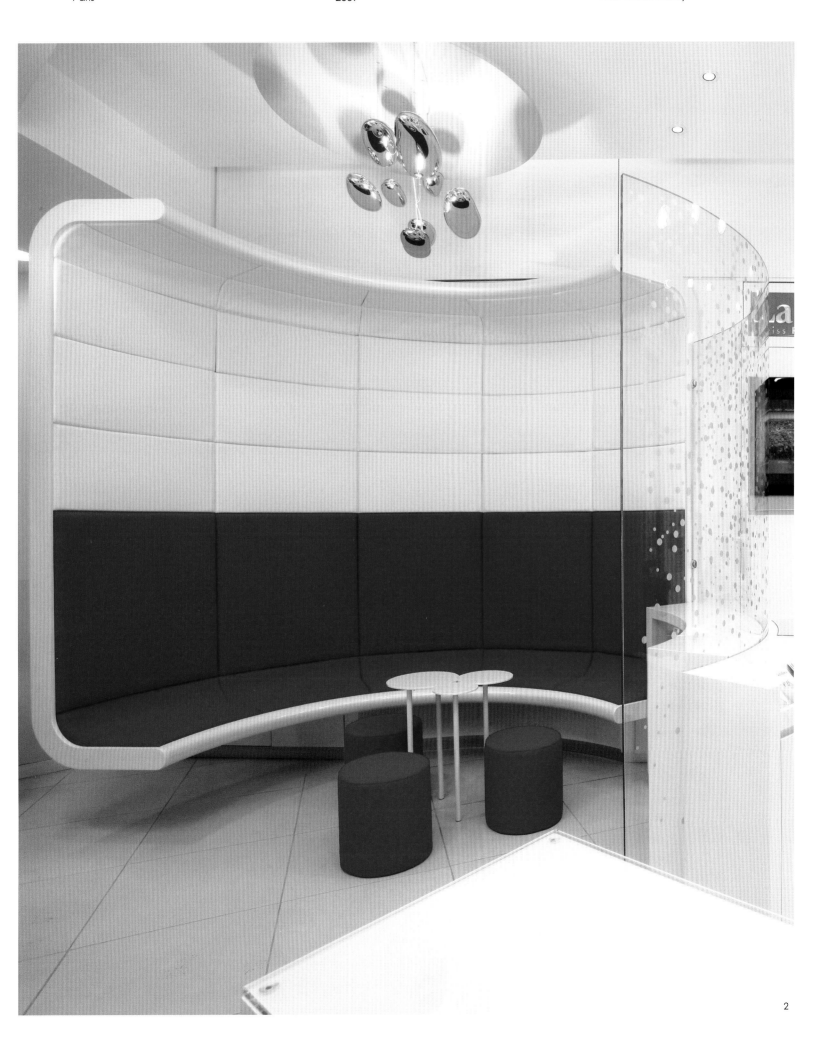

1. Overall view – reception space and shop window
2. Staircase

1. Treatment room
2. Below ground treatment rooms

Designer
Trio Ingénierie / Philippe Blanc

1

Les Anges ont la Peau Douce

Les Anges ont la Peau Douce ("Angels have Soft Skin") is a new concept in high end express beauty treatments, in glamorous and elegant surroundings. A vast "open lounge" in celestial blue, this place borrows the formula of New York express nail bars and gives it a very Parisian design and decoration. Half boutique, half beauty bar, this salon revisits the concept of the beauty institute. This place was born of a collaboration between Coralie Carbonell, the creator of the concept, and the architect Philippe Blanc, who specialises in projects for the fitting out of boutiques.

To start with, the door opens on the boutique part where the ranges of skincare products are presented. A central white lacquered block, very minimalist, shows off the products. It is set off by a series of hanging lamps with Wedgwood blue gathered shades, evoking softness and elegance. Next comes the treatment space, symbolically separated by a screen in the same blue tones.

This demarcation allows one to glimpse the entrance while preserving a certain privacy here. It is composed of five treatment stations, which are fully fledged modules: at each one a Cassina Dodo chair designed by Toshiyuki Kita faces a console and mirror that revisits the dressing tables of the past. These chairs, with their enveloping design, create a kind of cocoon for the client as they receiving the treatment. The modular nature of this chair is of the essence: it folds, unfolds and reclines according to one's wishes. On the consoles stand simple lamps with metallic bases, topped with the same blue gathered lampshades that are found all over the salon. Les Anges ont la Peau Douce is the mixture of a modern and understated environment punctuated with elements that are more baroque and bluish, which give the place its aerial and celestial identity.

1. Boutique space of the Beauty Lounge
2. Treatment space of the Beauty Lounge

Location
Paris

Completion Date
2010

Photographer
Coralie Carbonell

1. Treatment couch for face, hands and feet
2. Waiting area for the body treatment room
3. Plan
4. Treatment space seen from the boutique

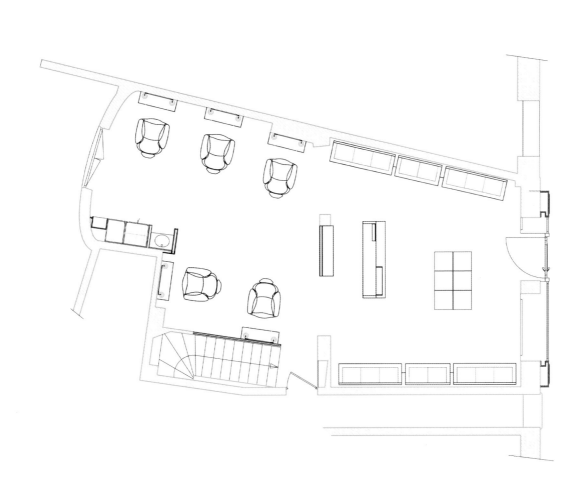

3

4

Les Alcôves de Valérie Guedj

The aim of the design of the "alcôves" space is to express the idea of an interior containing several intimate "niches" – the alcoves – with unique characteristics that describe the different uses linked to the work stations: the treatment space, the colour space, the technical (diagnosis) space, the hair space, the sales space, the function spaces (cloakroom, etc.).

From the stylistic point of view, the design of the space takes into account a certain form of intimacy, of relaxation, of wellbeing, close to a protective "home", while highlighting the natural aspect of the biosthetic products used. The visual identity as a whole aims to sensitise a new clientele, younger, urban, in search of wellbeing and relaxation, but also to differentiate the spaces for hair styling and traditional treatments, which are often uniform. An invitation is created to enter into a place imbued with a feeling of looking inward, in which to take care of oneself.

It must also come across as a refined, urban and chic space, with a contemporary and "seventies-retro" ambiance, but always in search of the natural and of wellbeing.

Photographs are used to set the scene via a single heroine, a young, flamboyant and sophisticated redhead, with a silhouette that changes as she moves freely through nature, in search of herself... Like a kind of plant road-movie, a hymn to nature, highlighted by a framing borrowed from the worlds of cinema and the senses, invites one to wander in a dream.

1. Reception area
2. Reception area seen through shop window

Location
Lyon

Completion Date
2008

Photographer
Alice dans les Villes

1. Welcome desk, cloak room and styling station
2. 3-D plan
3. View from the welcome desk

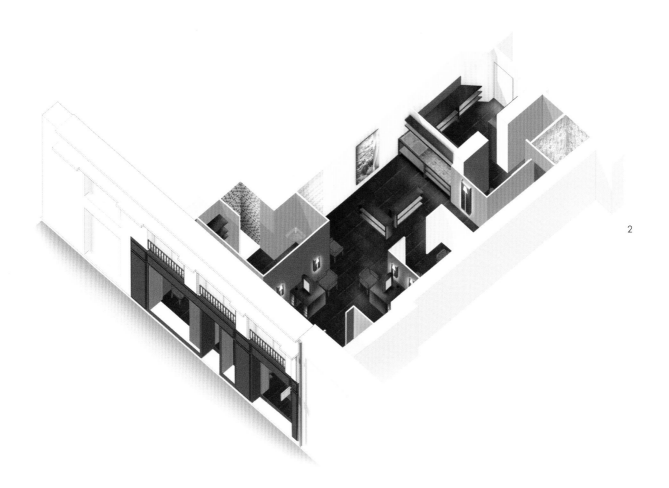

2

3

1. Cloak room
2. Hair colouring alcove
3. Hair colouring space
4. 3-D drawing

alcôves

1. Sink detail
2. Shampoo and rinse station
2. Signage of the hair styling space

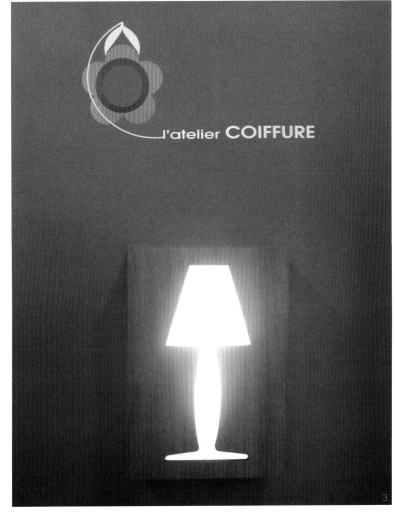

l'atelier COIFFURE

Alexandre Zouari

Alexandre Zouari has transformed the spirit of his Parisian salon calling on his own inspiration, rethinking it in order to create an intimate ambiance for a return to true values and to offer a more privileged relationship with each client.

Situated on the very beautiful Avenue du Président Wilson, this 250m² space opens towards the exterior thanks to eight large windows. A huge chandelier in Murano glass designed by Alexandre Zouari majestically lights the entrance to the salon which melts into a world of 18th-century grey, silver, white and black, the whole surrounded by mirrors to allow the brilliance and luminosity to shine.

Armchairs from the previous decor have been re-upholstered to Monsieur Zouari's exacting standards in black leather and pearlised grey. They surround white wooden consoles in black marble topped with mirrors with white rope frames lit by silvered bell lamps, echoing the curtain tiebacks. The salon is also lit by small silvery spotlights giving a starry effect. The black slate-effect floor transforms this salon into an artistic and ultra modern workshop where creation, expertise and wellbeing come together. This alliance of sparkling colours allows the clients to better appreciate the Zouari effect.

1. The building and awning of Alexandre Zouari
2. Salon entrance
3. Murano glass chandelier at the entrance

Location
Paris

Completion Date
2010

Photographer
Grégory Bozec

1-2. Hair styling space on the Avenue du Président Wilson
side of the salon
3. Conversation chair
4. Silvered bell lamps

2

3

4

1. Double dressing table in the colour space
2. Colour space seen from the shampooing area
3. Colour space

1. Kéraskin face and body beauty treatment room
2. Make-up console
3. Cloakroom access
4. Conversation chair

1

...by Katie Nat

Every architect has their own philosophy, their own vision of the world. But it's only right that this should be passed through the filter of the inner personality of their client. Katie Nat created this salon after fifteen years spent in the sanitised branches of the large luxury hair styling chains – far from her deep desires and aspirations.

A very personal world was therefore called for, very different from the archetypes that are current in the profession. A softened modernism, a heightened classicism? The aim was to create a cultivated space, capable of appealing to the sentimental background of each client. The plasterwork of the two rooms on the first floor were all that remained of the original decor of this apartment situated in a charming building from the beginning of the 19th century on a square in the centre of Toulouse. The whole place needed to be recreated: redistributing the volumes, installing a staircase, service areas, etc., but using an approach that interprets rather than copies in order to achieve a space of distinguished neutrality which aims more to convince than to dazzle.

Its success has been in reconciling a taste for discreet classicism with the curiosity of a collection of contemporary art and 20th century furniture, which are the pretext for showing her own and her friends' creations. The reception is in a square entrance hall with chalky-white walls set off by a simple painted wood panelling in the upper part where three strange terracotta busts look down from ceiling height. An oak point de Hongrie parquet is combined with a moiré effect carpet. It's a classic score played by an astonishing collection of furniture from the 40s to the 70s housing the accessories and beauty products. The staircase, in raw, blackened metal, leads to the first floor where padded doors in a grey-mauve fabric protect the facials room with its bird wallpaper and the treatment room. In the two white salons, clients can meet a friendly setting around large, post-neo-classical steel tables specially designed for the place.

1. Shop window in slate coloured wood and a screen covered in vintage fabric
2. The decor of the entrance has been created to fit with that of the first floor

Location
Toulouse

Completion Date
2009

Photographer
Marie & Daniel Suduca

1. Hair salons can be noisy but not here: all the doors have been padded to soften the acoustics
2. Simple shampooing stations with black leather seats and straight lines
3. First sketches, the spirit of the place
4. Products are displayed on the landing and double doors open onto several rooms
5. In a corner, a metal tree displays accessories

3

4

5

1. The original plasterwork has been preserved
2-3. The beauty treatment room has been lined in a hand-finished wallpaper

Designer
Alice dans les Villes
Clarisse Garcia & Jean-Christophe Bouvier

Cut by Marc Tavoukdjian

CUT: the cut – the break – the difference. Breaking with the traditional aesthetic codes. In correlation with a young and urban clientele, trendy and keen on fashion, the aim of the design as a whole and the work on the interior fit-out is to position the job of hair stylist not as the simple technical skill of the "cut", but as a revealer, a creator of identity/ies: to awaken the new personality that is hidden inside.

From an architectural and scenographical point of view, the fit-out of the space is based on the idea of a "minimalist Japanese box": the entire decor gives the effect of a box and its lid, from the interiors to the facade. A fuchsia "cutting line" runs through the whole space to divide it into two chromatic zones – white and "sugared-almond pink" – filling the height of the walls. The photographic characters are full-frontal, thus confidently assuming their new identity, a flower placed on the mouth...

From a graphic point of view, several imaginary characters, life-size and face-to-face with the client, punctuate the space, framing each hair-styling station. They are crossed by the cutting line at mid-chest level. The upper part, in graphic black and white, illustrates the hair matter in an almost abstract way, like the rough shape of the cut taking form. The lower part, representing the character's future new identity emerging, becomes coloured in fluorescent and acid colours, in harmony with the graphic chart and the colour codes of the cosmetic products used in the salon.

1. Detail of the façade, with view of the intérieur
2-3. Hair styling stations and decor

Location
Lyon

Completion Date
2007

Photographer
Alice dans les Villes

3

1. Shampooing area
2. Ceiling detail, reception area
3. Giant portraits for the interior decor
4. Working plan

2

3

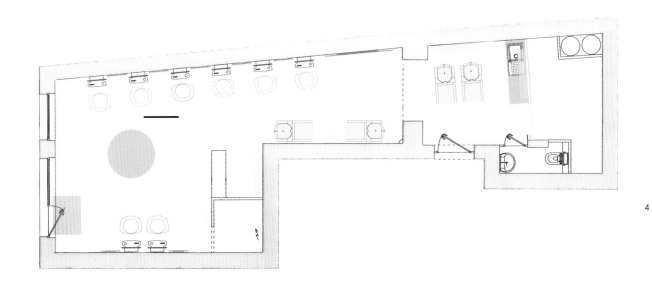

4

1. Child and baby area
2. Close-up of the children's and adults' spaces

BED HEAD

020 8338 1300

TIGI

David Mallett

In the recently enlarged David Mallett hair salon in the heart of Paris, clients feel a real change is in the air. Both luxurious and incredibly relaxing, this vast 17th-century apartment offers the perfect environment for a consultation, hair styling and exceptional care: it is more about intimacy than exclusivity.

In doubling its space to cover an area of more than 360m², the new look salon surrounds a green terrace open to the sky. The new wing of the salon has been furnished in David Mallett's own distinctive style: half flea market finds, half high concept design, it strikes the balance between elegance and a very welcoming environment. Lamps from Brussels stand beside sofas from Milan and a vintage sideboard from New York. A Tanzanian leopard shares the space with a majestic South African ostrich, both stuffed of course! The walls in soft taupe and the modern and angular work zones are juxtaposed with long and elegant windows.

"The style of the place is eclectic, chic and simple," explains Mallett. "It's a collection of objects from the past twenty years of my life, spent travelling the world, absorbing ideas and experiences."

1. White peacocks dominate the second hair styling room
2. Babeth, the lifesize stuffed ostrich

Location
Paris

Completion Date
2007

Photographer
Cyrille Groubé

1. The salon nestles in a 17th-century hôtel particulier
2. "A typical apartment, decorated by a typical Australian guy" as David Mallett himself describes it

1. Custom-made hair styling stations in brushed metal
2. Mallett's distinctive style: half flea market, half high concept design
3. The hand care and beauty space

2

3

1. Details of the shampooing room
2. A refined world reflecting the David Mallett style
3. An eclectic style, chic and simple

Jean-Claude Biguine – Paradis Road

After ten years in existence, the salon on Marseille's rue Paradis deserved a real rejuvenating treatment. In 2007, following the creation of the Jean-Claude Biguine house of beauty, situated not far from here on the Avenue du Prado, and in a fervor of creative energy, a complete refit of this prestigious hair care salon was undertaken.

The project retains the same purity of lines, accentuating horizontal tensions through the play of reflections, brilliance and through the lighting cleverly hidden behind the mirrors.

It would, besides, be more apt to speak of just a single mirror, twelve metres long, of a single magisterial gesture, structuring the space like a blade. The elegance of the whole is born of the alternation in the surfaces, now mat, now extremely shiny, and of the omnipresence of reflections, convergence lines and lighting which all direct the gaze to the universal and timeless symbol of beauty that is represented by the Birth of Venus, painted by the illustrious Botticelli.

1. View of the Botticelli Venus
2. Play of light and reflections

Location
Marseille

Completion Date
2008

Photographer
Thierry Lombardi

1. Cosmetic presentation units
2. Hair styling space
3. Plan

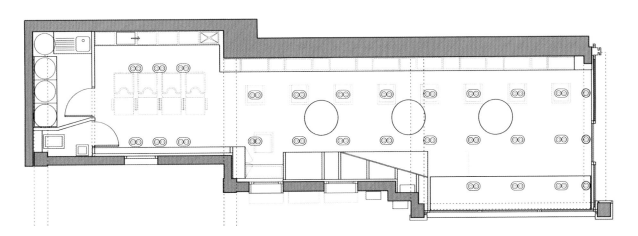

La Biosthétique

The architecture of La Biosthétique salons is an extension of the philosophy of its founders, and reflects their professional competence in all the domains of Total Beauty.

It is an architecture that marries the old and the modern. The historic facade of the Haussmannian building here offers an attractive contrast with the interior of the salon, which has a pared down style, a light and luminous world with simple geometric lines. The furniture and the decoration are of the highest quality and use noble materials. The refinement thus created is the perfect expression of the company's philosophy.

The exterior facade is pierced by three large windows, a symbol of openness and transparency which creates a magnificent visual link between the exterior and the interior and vice-versa. The rooms are long and thin, and cubic elements structure the space in a generous way. An impression of simple and sober elegance is obtained through the arrangement of the windows, flat surfaces, alignments and through the colour white which serves as a federating element and which is dressed up only by small touches of black and pearl.

1. La Biosthétique beauty salon: design and functionality at the highest level
2. Capillary care and colour space

Location
Paris

Completion Date
2007

Photographer
Nils Hendrik Müller

1

1. Cutting, colour and sales space
2. Stand-alone sinks for a private ambiance
3. Beauty and spa space bringing together luxury and wellbeing

2

3

Medley Rive Droite

At the end of a flower-filled courtyard, the Parisian salon Medley stands out for its originality. Arranged over two floors, this 240m² space was conceived by the American designer Peter Stelzner in the spirit of a New York loft. Straight away one discovers an intimate entrance, with a reception hall separated from the main room by windows framed in white wood which let the light pass through and conserve the perspective of the place. Next comes the main room, an open space covering 120m² under 4m high ceilings and a large glass skylight that bathes the whole of the ground floor in light.

A staircase in raw metal leads to the lower ground floor, which is a more cosy area with soft lighting. An invisible door blending into the wooden partition opens onto the private part of the salon: the colourist's laboratory, lingerie from organic materials, etc.

The furniture has been designed in a precious wood from Chile in a neo-classical style with impressive volumes and soft, rounded forms: dressing table-cabins like a sugarloaf, the reception desk at the entrance like a Roman chariot, and a huge set of wall shelves for an illuminated display of hair products. Metal furniture with an openwork design "recycled" from a post office sorting room also serve as display case for make-up. The hair-styling blocks have been cleverly mounted on casters to make the space modular. Their electrical light cables are deliberately visible, connected to the ceiling around the skylight. The materials clash and consolidate each other, the metal of the beams and structures, the aged and raw concrete of the floor, the slate of the shelves and the wood of the furniture combine forces for a very contemporary result, a cosmopolitan and urban place where the mix of genres is like Medley itself, always listening to the other person…

1. Salon entrance looking through to the main room lit by a large skylight
2. The mobile styling stations which allow one to modify the space at will, and their leather chairs

Location
Paris

Completion Date
2007

Photographer
Frédéric Cresseaux

1. Bar of slate and metal beams in the relaxation space
2. Pierced metal postal sorting shelves are used to display products on sale
3. Furniture in precious wood with feminine forms is bathed in light from the skylight
4. The beauty and image consulting space with a view of the flower-filled courtyard

3

4

Designer
Michel Freudiger (architecture)
Patrick Ahmed (decoration)

1

Medley Rive Gauche

Born of an avant-garde concept with English influences thrown into the mix, and today reflecting its creator Patrick Ahmed, Medley Rive Gauche is a pleasant and welcoming space organised around wellbeing where different genres come together.

The Medley Rive Gauche salon is above all a design space that's all about luminosity, recalling cinema studio dressing rooms, which were a marvellous source of inspiration. The structure of the salon itself dates from the end of the 1950s, with an original staircase and armchairs. Its style is both sober and flashy, its decor mixing minimalist and ethnic effects. And furniture in the colour of "Smarties", a mosaic floor and walls fitted with carpentry break with the clichés of traditional hair salons.

The simple and functional space allows one to organise the services wisely, with shampooing, treatments and personalised care on the first floor, all accompanied by a gentle massage while the specialists treat and colour the hair. The consultation with the hair stylist takes place on the ground floor in a bare space where plasma video screen and lounge music enhance this moment of relaxation.

1. View from the stairs
2. Hair styling station on the ground floor

Location
Paris

Completion Date
2005

Photographer
Sam Pagel

1. A 70s spirit and plasma screens lend energy to the walls
2. Shelves displaying hair-styling products, a combination of different styles and colours
3. The armchairs date from the 1950s

1

2

1. A huge storage unit gives a sense of rhythm to the shop window
2. Small display table and shelves giving onto the shop window
3-4. Details of the window display in the salon, unexpected companions…

1. Staircase leading to the first floor
2-3. Details of the 50s banister

1. Arrival at the first floor
2. The sinks on the first floor and shelves mixing hair care
   products and African statuettes
3. Space dedicated to treatments and personalised care

2

3

Mum & Babe

Mum & Babe has benefitted from the creation of an interior architecture at the same time as the creation of the brand. Besides the imperatives of functionality and use, the place has been designed from a standpoint of escaping from any preconceived ideas of a hair salon. Thus, from the window to the salon via the children's space and the treatment rooms, well-being, confidence and creativity are worked through the bias of spaces, colours, materials and the sensory aliveness of the place.

Exchange, warmth and conviviality gather around the large styling table, conceived in the style of a communal dining table and overhung by a huge mobile, a shimmering and moving sky that calms mothers and fascinates their children. The space is treated in a light and reassuring way: the visitor knows where she is, and visualises the place where her child is while being distinctly removed from it.

The children's space is in fact the heart of the salon, a large window allowing them to follow the play and activities of their offspring. This architectural membrane recalls the architectural history of the 11th arrondissement of Paris and its workshops. Colour, materials and light are worked in a confident way, codifying the place and accompanying the movement given by the giant mobile. All the elements are linked to each other, creating the uniqueness and the signature of this project with appropriateness and harmony.

1. Hair salon
2. Hair washing stations

Location
Paris

Completion Date
2009

Photographer
Rebecka Oftedal

1-2. Hair salon and the glass screen of the children's area

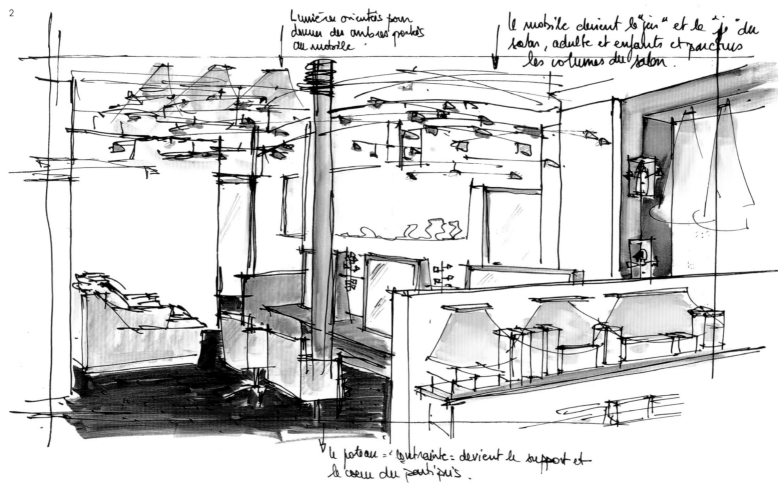

1. Hair salon
2. Preparatory drawing
3. Communicating beauty treatment rooms
4. Layout plan and 3-D drawing

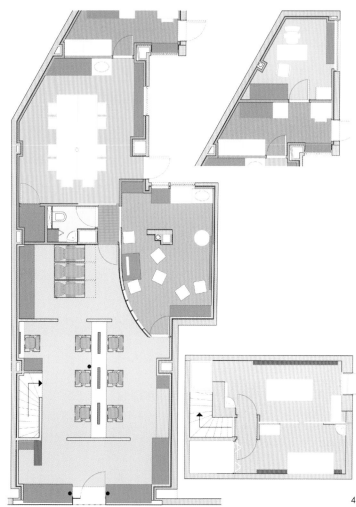

La Nouvelle Athènes

After more than 17 years spent in photographic studios and behind the scenes at fashion shows, Sylvie Coudray took up the challenge of creating a hair salon whose essence is a made-to-measure service and well-being. At La Nouvelle Athènes the key word is Harmony.

La Nouvelle Athènes nestles in a cosy apartment in the very chic ninth *arrondissement*. Thus baptised in reference to this quarter with its architecture inspired by Antiquity, whose 19th-century salons brought together the artists and writers of the time, La Nouvelle Athènes has in four years become an established address that is both intimate and welcoming, and an artistic meeting place where artists, painters, photographers and sculptors expose their creations.

Out of respect for this neighbourhood and for the comfort of her visitors, Sylvie Coudray has chosen to renovate the Napoleon III style of this superb apartment. The gilding, the parquets and the fireplaces have just been repatinated to retain the traces of time and its history. The choice of colours was inspired by Venetian palaces. Sky blue is very present in the salons of La Nouvelle Athènes, giving them a luminous and soft character. The boudoir ambiance is led by the gilding and the red velvet that envelops the cosy sofas. Each decorative element, from the rugs to the sofas and low tables, has been collected from flea markets and antique shops to grace this place with their history. Everything is done so that each visitor has the pleasant sensation of arriving in a warm and welcoming place, far from the bustle outside.

1. Waiting room
2. Perspective

Location
Paris

Completion Date
2003

Photographer
Serge Rameli

1

1-2. Main cutting salon
3. View from the entrance
4. Light fitting

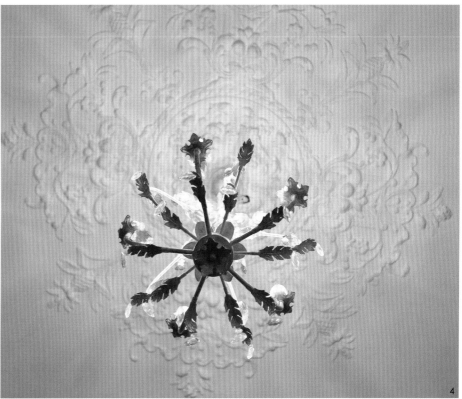

1. A salon
2-3. Premier cutting salon

Patrice Renouard Versailles

Situated in Paris, near the Maison de la Radio, this salon was to be renovated to offer a new image that was both youthful and welcoming. This first project would serve as a shop window for a future chain of salons aiming to offer its clientele a place of relaxation and comfort.

Colours and materials play a major role in creating the "cosy" atmosphere sought for this salon. The floor has been covered with chocolate coloured ceramic tiles with an appearance of leather to create a feeling of comfort and of being at home. The colours orange and bronze bring a touch of freshness to the whole.

The 120m² salon is made up of four main zones: the reception, men's and women's hair styling, the shampooing area and a private salon that groups together massage and relaxation spaces.

The general organisation of the salon favours a fluid movement that is intuitive for clients. All the furniture situated in the hair styling space is mobile in order to offer the freedom to arrange it according to the needs of the salon. A line of low pieces of furniture marks out the contours of this zone and allows for the hair stylists' materials to be tidied away. Each piece of furniture has been made to order so as to match perfectly the general ambiance of the place. Special attention has been paid to the hair-styling units. Their U-shaped form allows one to create a kind of cocoon around the client, offering him or her a real sense of privacy.

1. Reception and waiting area
2. Women's zone and waiting area

Location
Paris

Completion Date
2008

Photographer
Nicolas Fussler

1-2. Waiting area
3. Styling station
4. Women's and men's zones
5. Plan

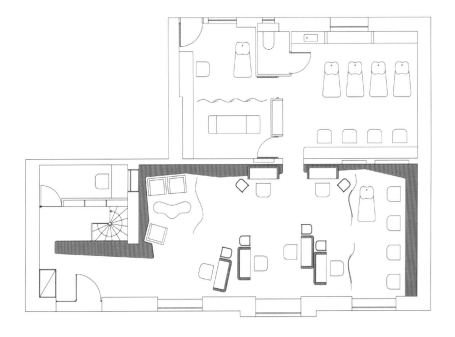

5

1-2. Men's zone
3. Shampooing space

Designer
Alice dans les Villes
Clarisse Garcia & Jean-Christophe Bouvier

Préciosa

To work colour, cuts, skincare, body care, make-up, in a small space of 45m² is possible! Optimising the space by creating centres of intimacy in which the client feels at home, sits down confidently and lets "time fly".

A marriage of precious materials, sometimes natural, sometimes raw, appears, like sophisticated touches, a relationship between the matt and the gloss, refinement of the colours in a subtle patchwork of neutrals, hot colours, sand and marron glacé with a dissonant touch of turquoise. The space has here been sculpted like hair to create a subtle atmosphere, an accumulation of objects like in a dolls' house, mannerist and quirky settings, a space that seems radiant with light, deceptively uncluttered.

Each work point has its styling station, single or double, delicately stylised and reminiscent "of a sleeping beauty" of today. Each zone (treatment or make-up room, cloakroom...) is punctuated by a change of wall decoration, giving the impression of waking up in the middle of a dream... The photographic work aims to create imaginary characters with "invented" hairstyles in the style of illustrations from the Perrault fairytales, or from Slavic or Nordic folklore.

1. General view from outside the shop window
2. Close-up of two single hair-styling stations

Location
Lyon

Completion Date
2008

Photographer
Alice dans les Villes

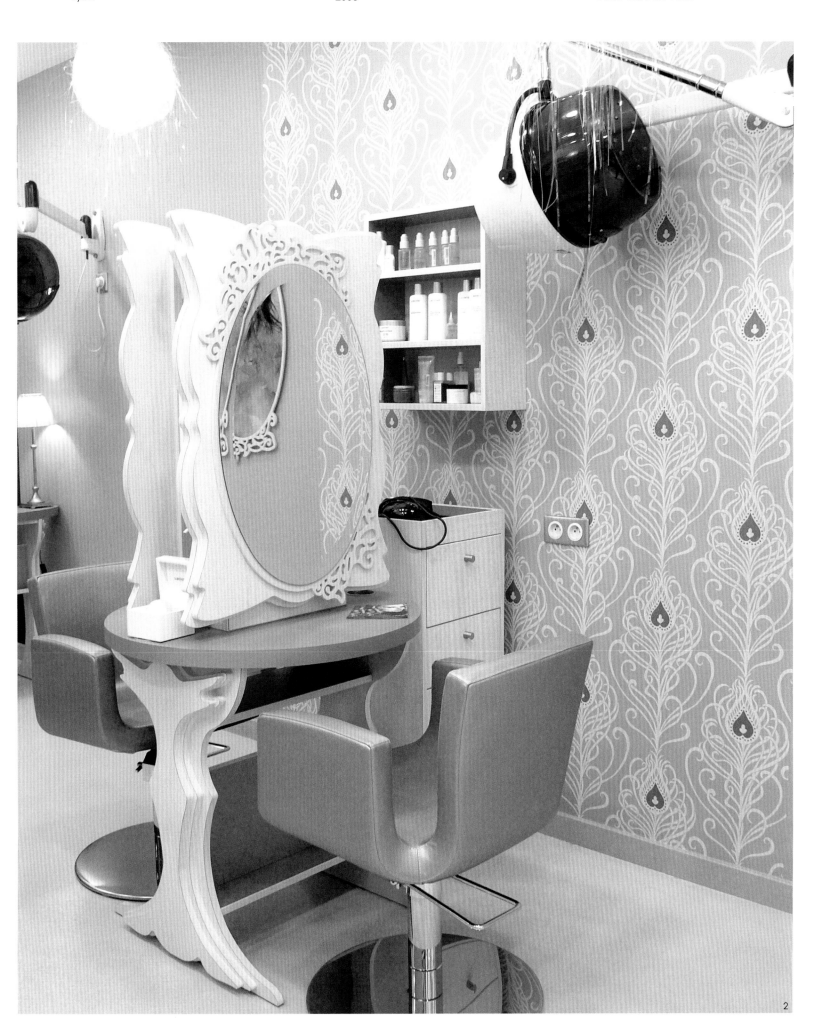

1. Research for the interior decoration and visual identity
2. Double hair-styling station
3. Axonometry of the salon

2

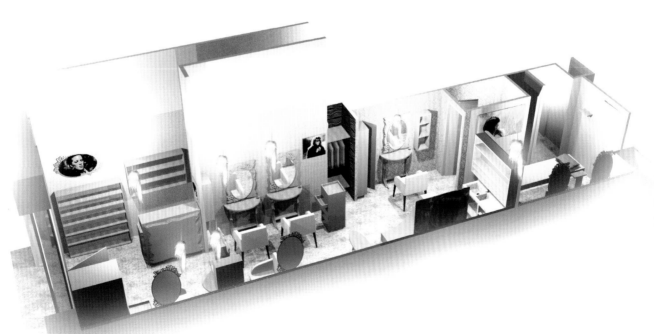

3

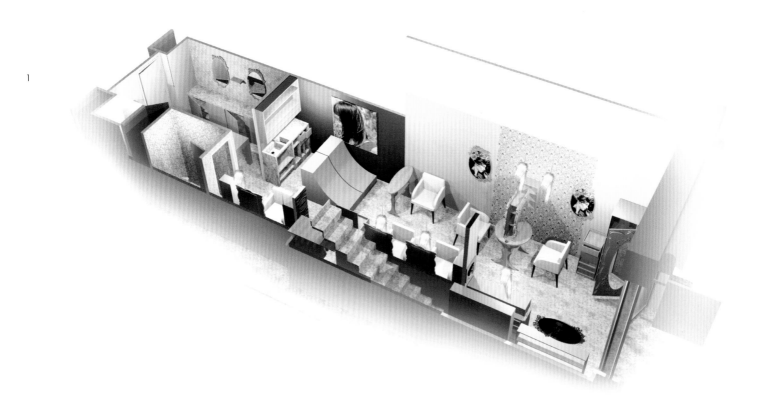

1

2

1. Axonometry of the salon
2. Detail of the body treatment room
3. Body treatment room
4. Detail of the fitting out of the WC

Designer
Jacques Rival
Karl Nawrot

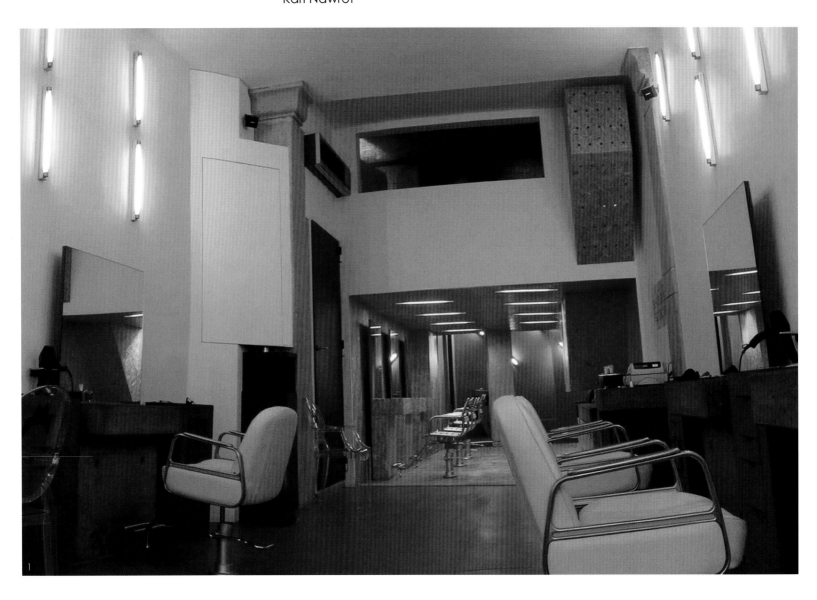

Second Face

The redesigned hair salon wanted to keep the soul that it has always had since its opening: a place created to provide a musical and multi-faceted experience, as well as offering a unique and powerful architectural habitat.

The project is focused on three different spaces in terms of function and presentation and is mapped out by a grid system executed by three measurements – 72cm x 72cm and by ratio of 2/3 – 1/3. There is a refined and contrasting welcome area constructed of concrete for the dressing console tables, an anthracite black floor, white walls and individually mounted lights, which provides rhythm to the entrance of the salon as well as functioning as a light installation. The technical space is set apart from the entrance by warmer and less noble material: Triply. It covers the floors and walls as well as the suspended stairs leading up to the mezzanine, which forms a built-in sculpture.

Walking through the salon provides a contrasting and changing experience thanks to the use of completely different materials while reincorporating the already existing furniture. The whole was conceived by an architect and a typographer-designer working with a foreman who wanted a sharply defined workplace in terms of design.

1. Sculptural hair styling space, the grille lighting system
2. Triply OSB (exterior board) enveloping the technical space and the lighting system

1. Access to the mezzanine: the pierced Triply lighting box
2. The Triply OSB envelope on two levels
3. The suspended staircase

3

Designer
Jacques Rival

Second Face Workshop

In the direct line of the first Second Face salon, a new workshop was created. Even if the project keeps the original concept of a multi-experience place, it spreads over two fronts: the street side and the courtyard side. The space is based around a line of dressing tables and a water technical block, a strong perspective emphasised by an inclined-plane ceiling leading to the courtyard. The courtyard then stands as a colorful background to close the space.

The working tables are treated like boxes in an IPN project so as to stress the object appearance of the whole and differentiate them from the concrete floor-map. The white concrete dressing tables mimic the table design that exists within the first Second Face salon. The simple and technical lighting stresses the interior concept which is at the same time directing and decorative. The whole lighting is plain and minimal, emphasising a warm atmosphere.

1. A line of white concrete styling stations on a quartz base
2. Container and the inclined plane on a coloured background

1. Styling and technical prowess brought together in a
   single dynamic
2. White concrete styling station with mirror
3. The WCs are hidden in the container
4. Plan

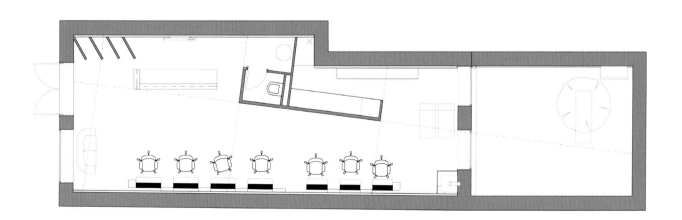

Seran Faugères

Situated in a bourgeois apartment in the heart of Toulouse, the Seran Faugères beauty space offers a very private space to a select clientele. Its owners wanted to break with the codes established by traditional salons and to offer their clients a warmer and less conventional atmosphere. As the initial volumes could not be modified, this former residential apartment had to be reappropriated to transform it into a real work tool that fulfilled all the technical and practical demands.

The essential idea of the project was to make the most of the existing spaces by combining their classicism with a modernity brought by subtle touches. Two hair styling spaces have been defined, connected by a waiting room organised around a fireplace. The first space had a more sober aspect thanks to its panelling and mouldings. Sober and elegant furniture made to order mixes with this classicism, creating a pure and sophisticated sheath. On the ceiling, one is attracted by the graphic presence of a hair sculpture that runs across it and adds a contemporary touch.

The whole apartment has been painted in powdery white struck through with lines of fluorescent pink with different widths, marrying all the details like a kind of ribbon that wraps up the space. The contrast of the 19th-century decorative elements with these bands of shocking colours and marked directions assures this new space the desired modernity!

1. Relaxation salon
2. Hair styling space
3. Styling stations

Location
Toulouse

Completion Date
2009

Photographer
Ha Mind Duy

1. Waiting room
2. Shampooing and capillary treatment space
3. Lighting
4. Shampooing sinks

2

3

4

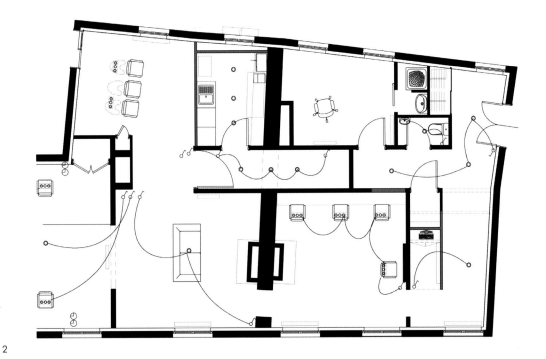

1. Plan
2. Mirrors opening up the space
3. Circulation corridor

Toni&Guy The Guild

The Montorgueil quarter in Paris is the fiefdom of designers, and in 2003 Philippe Gentner opens his salon here. While remaining part of the group, the Toni&Guy The Guild salon is to have its own identity and its own concept. The tone is set; the salon will be "underground" in silver-grey and white shades with a very hip musical ambiance.

In 2009, the salon is six years old. Change is in the air! Philippe Gentner wants to make it evolve, to mix old and modern in a chic and designer aesthetic without it looking like a fashion. Black is the dominant colour. To avoid a feeling of sombreness, a shiny, reflective Plexiglas is introduced with sober, very contemporary forms. In counterpart, period-style ceiling mouldings have been created in concrete. The association of these two worlds brings softness and elegance. The mirror effects installed all along the main space offer original visual perspectives. Large tiles, also with a mirror effect, have been placed on the floor. A subtle chocolatey tone blends into the nuances and goes together perfectly with the grey concrete and the black.

Everything has been redone and thought out with the wellbeing of the client and the team in mind. The furniture has been chosen with great care to combine elegance and comfort. The 60s pop influenced chairs in white and black leather are ample and pleasant to sit in. The old lightbulbs have ceded their place to energy-saving models. At the shopfront, the combination of the Toni&Guy logo and two mouldings representing the seal of the company offers a nice foretaste of the interior style.

1. Shampooing space and luminous product display shelves
2. Colouring and chromotherapy space

Location
Paris

Completion Date
2009

Photographer
Edouard de Blay

1. Main thoroughfare of the salon seen from the entrance
2. Relaxation and massage space. Chromotherapy sinks

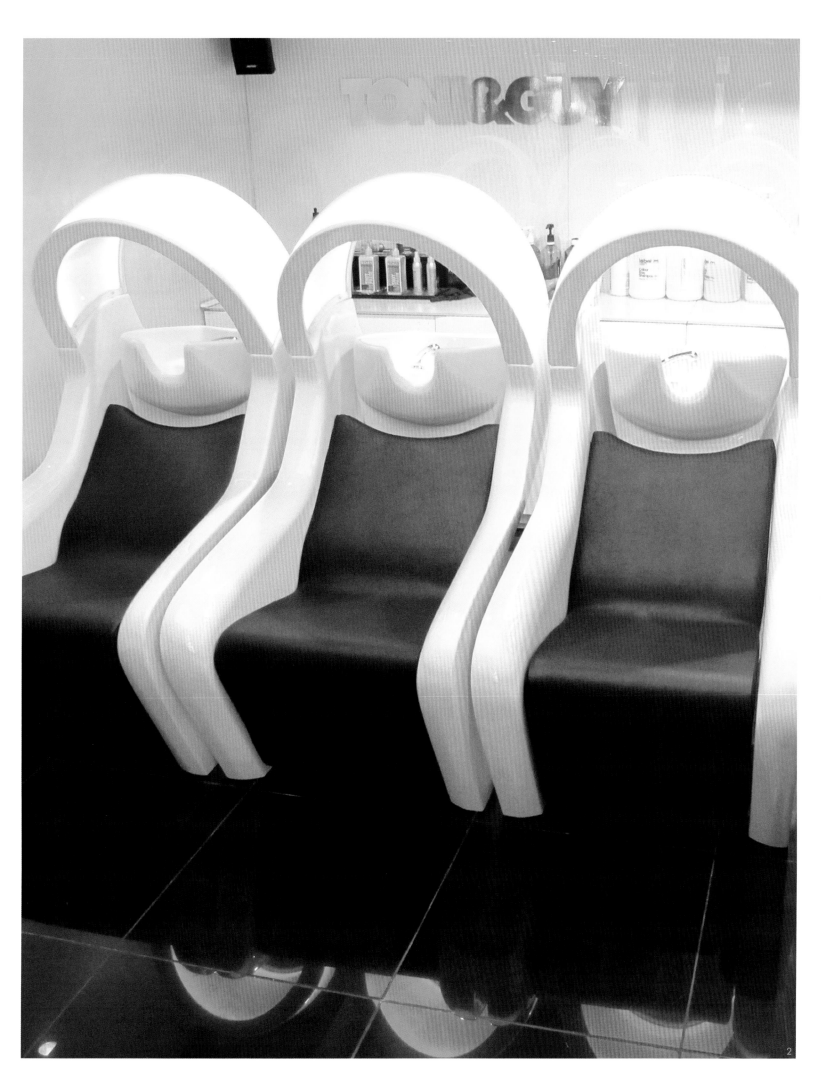

David Lucas en Aparté

No designer of the moment, no star decorator for this unusual hair salon, just a taste for beautiful things and master of the house David Lucas's incurable desire to receive his clients somewhere where each one will feel at home. Here, everything is beautiful, elegant, comfortable and peaceful. With the help of friends, experts and professionals who offered their good advice, David Lucas stepped into the project manager's shoes for five months! His choice fell on a second floor, close to the sumptuous Place Vendôme, and there a series of craftsmen intent on creating beauty followed one another relentlessly to transform this apartment into a hair salon, with the aim of bringing out the soul of this authentic Parisian apartment as its guiding line.

High ceilings are thus decorated with majestic mirrors sourced by David Lucas himself, the original parquets have been carefully preserved, just renovated, the walls are covered with beautiful contemporary colours. Then, just beside the attractive hair styling seats chosen from an important Italian designer, you find antique furniture, sourced by David with the precious advice of LiLa K at the famous Paris flea market of Saint-Ouen. The lights, custom made by Adélaïde de Ponchalon, marry the volumes of the rooms and the colours of the walls in a warm harmony.

On the technical side, at David Lucas you relax during treatments in comfortable massage chairs placed in front of the pure lines of the sinks, all chosen from an Italian designer. Finally, each week the vases by the celebrated Djordje Varda are filled with majestic orchids.

1. Sofa in the reception room
2. Reception room

Location
Paris

Completion Date
2010

Photographer
Yoan Gari

1. Product ranges in the reception room
2. View towards the technical room
3. Main salon

David_ucas
en aparté

1. Styling station in the main salon
2. Antique storage chest used for accessories in the main salon
3. Styling table in the main salon

Index of Projects-Establishments

Alexandre Zouari
1 avenue du Président Wilson 75116 Paris
T+33 (0)1 47 23 79 00
contact@alexandre-zouari.com
www.alexandre-zouari.com

Anne Fontaine Spa
370 rue Saint-Honoré 75001 Paris
T+33 (0)1 42 61 03 70
spa@annefontaine.com
www.annefontaine.com

Aquensis
Rue du Pont d'Arras 65200 Bagnères de Bigorre
T+33 (0)5 62 95 86 95
F+33 (0)5 62 95 11 41
info@aquensis-bagneres.com
www.aquensis.fr

Audebert Institute
88 Boulevard Saint-Germain 75005 Paris
T+33 (0)1 44 07 20 28
F+33 (0)1 46 34 14 76
audebert@gmail.com

Biologique Recherche
32 avenue des Champs-Élysées 75008 Paris
T+33 (0)1 41 18 96 84
info@biologique-recherche.com
www.biologique-recherche.com

...by Katie Nat
2 place Rouaix 31000 Toulouse
T+33 (0)5 62 17 08 49
contact@bykatienat.com

Boscolo Exedra Nice Hotel
12 boulevard Victor Hugo 06000 Nice
T+33 (0)4 97 03 89 89
F+33 (0)4 93 88 68 60
reception@exedranice.boscolo.com
www.boscolohotels.com

Carita House of Beauty
11 rue du Faubourg Saint-Honoré 75008 Paris
T+33 (0)1 44 94 11 11
maisondebeaute@carita.fr
www.carita.fr

Carlota Institute
16 avenue Hoche 75008 Paris
T+33 (0)1 42 89 42 89
www.institutcarlota.com

Cinq Mondes Brussels
Dolce La Hulpe Brussels
135 Chaussée de Bruxelles 1310 La Hulpe, Belgium
T+32 (0)2 290 99 01
cinq.mondes@dolce.com
www.dolce-la-hulpe-brussels-hotel.com

Cinq Mondes Paris
6 square de l'Opéra Louis Jouvet 75009 Paris
T+33 (0)1 42 66 00 60
www.cinqmondes.com

Clé des Champs
113 rue Duguesclin 69006 Lyon
T+33 (0)4 37 241 241
contact@cledeschamps.eu
www.cledeschamps.eu

Cotton'Spa
Colonial Country Club
Vieux Chemin de Paris 91450 Etioles
T+33 (0)1 69 89 90 00
contact@cotton-spa.com
www.cotton-spa.com

Cut by Marc Tavoukdjian
17 rue Childebert 69002 Lyon
T+33 (0)4 78 42 24 57
cut-by-marc-tavoukdjian@cut-by-marc-tavoukdjian.com
www.cut-by-marc-tavoukdjian.com

David Lucas en Aparté
20 rue Danielle Casanova 75002 Paris
T+33 (0)1 47 03 92 04
davidlucas75@hotmail.fr
www.davidlucas.fr

David Mallett
14 rue Notre-Dame des Victoires 75002 Paris
T+33 (0)1 40 20 00 23
F+33 (0)1 40 20 00 24
info@david-mallett.com
www.david-mallett.com

Dior Institut / Plaza Athénée
25 avenue Montaigne 75008 Paris
T+33 (0)1 53 67 65 35
institutdior@plaza-athenee-paris.com
www.plaza-athenee-paris.com

Diva Institute
16 rue Henri Provostic 29830 Ploudalmézeau
T+33 (0)2 98 48 06 63

Guerlain Spa
68 avenue des Champs-Élysées 75008 Paris
T+33 (0)1 45 62 11 21
www.guerlain.com

Harnn & Thann Spa
11 rue Molière 75001 Paris
T+33 (0)1 40 15 02 20
contact@harnn.fr
www.harnn.fr

Hotel Mont-Blanc
Place de l'Église 74120 Megève
T+33 (0)4 50 21 20 02
F+33 (0)4 50 21 45 28
contact@hotelmontblanc.com
www.sibuethotels-spa.com

Jean-Claude Biguine – Paradis Road
444 rue Paradis 13008 Marseille
T+33 (0)4 91 71 74 51
F+33 (0)4 91 27 17 33
www.biguine.com

Jean-Claude Biguine – Prado Avenue
33 avenue du Prado 13006 Marseille
T+33 (0)4 91 37 72 35
F+33 (0)4 91 27 17 33
www.biguine.com

La Biosthétique
35 avenue Pierre 1er de Serbie 75008 Paris
T+33(0)1 56 64 03 10
info@coiffurebeaute-paris.com
www.labiosthetique.de

La Clairière
63 route d'Ingwiller 67290 La Petite Pierre
T+33 (0)3 88 71 75 00
F+33 (0)3 88 70 41 05
info@laclairiere.com
www.la-clairiere.com

La Colline Institute
24 avenue de l'Opéra 75001 Paris
T+33 (0)1 49 26 03 66
institut@lacolline-skincare.com
www.lacolline-skincare.com

La Nouvelle Athènes
46 rue Laffitte 75009 Paris
T+33 (0)1 48 74 86 89
contact@lanouvelleathenes.com
www.lanouvelleathenes.com

La Sultane de Saba
8 bis rue Bachaumont 75002 Paris
T+33 (0)1 40 41 90 95
F+33 (0)1 40 41 11 45
servicedepresse@lasultanedesaba.com
www.lasultanedesaba.com

Le Clos Saint-Martin
Cours Pasteur 17410 Saint-Martin-de-Ré
T+33 (0)5 46 01 10 62
F+33 (0)5 46 01 99 89
reservation@le-clos-saint-martin.com
www.le-clos-saint-martin.com

Les Alcôves de Valérie Guedj
90 rue de Créqui 69006 Lyon
T+33 (0)4 78 52 36 87

Les Anges ont la Peau Douce
254 rue du Faubourg Saint-Honoré 75008 Paris
T+33 (0)1 47 64 48 24
ccarbonell@lesangesontlapeaudouce.fr
www.lesangesontlapeaudouce.com

Les Fermes de Marie
Chemin de Riante Colline 74120 Megève
T+33 (0)4 50 93 03 10
F+33 (0)4 50 93 09 84
contact@fermesdemarie.com
www.fermesdemarie.com

Les Granges d'en Haut
Route des Chavants
Les Houches Chamonix
T+33 (0)4 50 54 65 36
F+33 (0)4 50 89 01 97
welcome@lodgemontagnard.com
www.grangesdenhaut.com

L'Espace Weleda
10 avenue Franklin D. Roosevelt 75008 Paris
T+33 (0)1 53 96 06 15
service.consommateur@weleda.fr
www.espace-weleda.fr

Lodge Park
100 rue d'Arly 74120 Megève
T+33 (0)4 50 93 05 03
F+33 (0)4 50 93 06 52
contact@lodgepark.com
www.sibuethotels-spa.com

Loreamar Thalasso Spa / Grand Hotel
43 boulevard Thiers 64500 Saint-Jean-de-Luz
T+33 (0)5 59 26 35 36
F+33 (0)5 59 51 99 84
reservation@luzgrandhotel.fr
www.luzgrandhotel.fr

Medley Rive Droite
21 rue Vieille du Temple 75004 Paris
T+33 (0)1 44 61 89 29
medleyrivedroite@yahoo.fr
www.medley.fr

Medley Rive Gauche
134 boulevard Raspail 75006 Paris
T+ 33 (0)1 43 26 17 59
rivegauche@medley.fr
www.medley.fr

Mum & Babe
3 rue Keller 75011 Paris
T+33 (0)1 43 38 83 55
contact@mumandbabe.fr
www.mumandbabe.fr

Nuxe
32 rue Montorgueil 75002 Paris
T+33 (0)1 42 36 65 65
accueil@nuxe.com
www.nuxe.com

Patrice Renouard Versailles
19 avenue de Versailles 75016 Paris
T+33 (0)1 45 24 57 57

Préciosa
131 rue Bugeaud 69006 Lyon
T+33 (0)4 78 24 64 76
pr-eciosa@hotmail.fr

Second Face
3 rue Mercière 69002 Lyon
T+33 (0)4 78 42 95 46
bruce.coulaux@wanadoo.fr

Second Face Workshop
109 boulevard de la Croix Rousse 69004 Lyon
T+33 (0)4 78 42 95 46
vanessa.coulaux@wanadoo.fr

Seran Faugères
2 rue d'Austerlitz 31000 Toulouse
T+33 (0)5 61 21 27 95
contact@seran-faugeres.com
www.seran-faugeres.com

Six Senses Spa
3 rue de Castiglione 75001 Paris
T+33 (0)143 16 10 10
T+33 (0)143 16 10 11
reservations-castiglione-spa@sixsenses.com
www.sixsenses.com

Spa Baumanière
Mas de Carita 13250 Les Baux de Provence
T+33 (0)4 90 54 24 67
infospa@maisonsdebaumaniere.com
www.maisonsdebaumaniere.com

Spa Comfort Zone
49 rue Quincampoix 75004 Paris
T+33 (0)1 44 78 64 64
spaquincamp@wanadoo.fr
www.spa-comfortzone.com

Spa des Neiges / Hotel Cheval Blanc Le Jardin Alpin
73121 Courchevel 1850
T+33 (0)79 00 50 50
F+33 (0)4 79 00 50 51
info@chevalblanc.com
www.chevalblanc.com

Spark
87 rue du Général de Gaulle 95880 Enghien-les-Bains
T+33 (0)1 39 34 10 50
F+33 (0)1 39 34 10 51
sparkenghien@lucienbarriere.com
www.lucienbarriere.com

Thémaé
20-22 rue Croix des Petits Champs 75001 Paris
T+33 (0)1 40 20 48 60
www.themae.fr

Thermes Marins de Cannes
47 rue Georges Clémenceau 06400 Cannes
T+33 (0)4 92 99 50 12
F+33 (0)4 92 99 50 11
reservations@lesthermesmarins-cannes.com
www.lesthermesmarins-cannes.com

Toni&Guy The Guild
18 rue Tiquetonne 75002 Paris
T+33 (0)1 40 41 11 00
toniandguy.tiquetonne@orange.fr
www.toniandguy.fr

Ultimate Spa / Château de Villiers-le-Mahieu
78770 Villiers-le-Mahieu
T+33 (0)1 34 87 44 25
F+33 (0)1 34 87 44 40
accueil@chateauvilliers.com
www.chateauvilliers.com

U Spa Barrière / Majestic Barrière
10 La Croisette 06400 Cannes
T+33 (0)4 92 98 77 49
majestic-spa@lucienbarriere.com
www.majestic-spa.com

Villa Thalgo
8 avenue Raymond Poincaré 75016 Paris
T+33 (0)1 45 62 00 20
F+33 (0)1 45 62 85 94
contact@villathalgo.com
www.villathalgo.com

Wellness Beauty
98 rue Duguesclin 69006 Lyon
T+33 (0)4 37 43 65 33
wellnessbeauty@free.fr
www.wellnessbeauty.fr

Index of Designers

Acra-Studio Sarl d'Architecture
18 rue de Richelieu 75001 Paris
T+33 (0)1 42 61 02 07
F+33 (0)1 42 61 54 60
acrastudio@gmail.com

A.D.N / PARIS
Architecture Design Nomade
47 rue d'Alsace 75010 Paris
T+33 (0)1 40 35 18 30
F+33 (0)1 40 35 18 30
contact@studioadn.fr
www.studioadn.fr

Alice dans les Villes
7 place Benoît Crépu 69005 Lyon
T+33 (0)4 78 42 03 81
F+33 (0)4 78 37 50 74
contact@alicedanslesvilles.com
www.alicedanslesvilles.com

A&MB
10 rue Mousset Robert 75012 Paris
T+33 (0)1 43 45 71 86
F+33 (0)1 43 45 20 30
annaik.barbe@a-mb.com
www.a-mb.com

Maryam Ashford-Brown
107 rue Molière 94200 Ivry-sur-Seine
T+33 (0)1 53 14 18 98
F+33 (0)1 46 71 51 50
atelier_14@yahoo.fr

Frédéric Bensemhoun
11 rue Molière 75001 Paris
T+33 (0)1 40 15 02 20
contact@harnn.fr
www.harnn.fr

Norman Binder
fmb Architekten
Stöckachstraße 16 D-70190 Stuttgart Germany
T+49 (07)11 614 26 91
F+49 (07)11 636 85 01
info@fmb-architekten.de
www.fmb-architekten.de

Christiane Broc / Cotton'Spa
Colonial Country Club Vieux Chemin de Paris
91450 Étioles
T+33 (0)1 69 89 90 00
contact@cotton-spa.com
www.cotton-spa.com

Centdegrés
10 rue Chauchat 75009 Paris
T+33 (0)1 44 72 59 00
F+33 (0)1 44 72 04 50
contact@centdegres.fr
www.centdegres.fr

Sylvie Coudray
46 rue Laffitte 75009 Paris
T+33 (0)1 48 74 86 89
contact@lanouvelleathenes.com
www.lanouvelleathenes.com

David & Lampros / Pierre David
7 rue Oberkampf 75011 Paris
T+33 (0)1 47 00 04 33
pierre.david@david-lampros.fr

DC&R / Catherine Diot-Clément & Florence Renouf
60 rue Fessart 92100 Boulogne-Billancourt
T+33 (0)1 46 04 10 63
contact@dcrparis.com
www.dcrparis.com

Marc Deloche
9 rue Antonin Mercié 31000 Toulouse
marcdeloche@aol.com
www.marc-deloche.com

Luc Demolombe Architecte
39 rue de Périole 31500 Toulouse
T+33 (0)5 61 48 72 77
F+33 (0)5 61 48 72 79
luc.demolombe@wanadoo.fr

Serge Deronne
11 rue François Dauphin 69002 Lyon
T+33 (0)6 63 16 92 86
serge.deronne@gmail.com

Pascal Desprez
30 avenue Marceau 75008 Paris
T+33 (0)1 47 20 10 23
F+33 (0)1 40 70 01 32
pascal.desprez@dp.agence.fr
www.dpagence.fr

Brigitte Dumont de Chassard / Latitudes
10 rue des Filles du Calvaire 75003 Paris
T+33 (0)1 40 27 85 01
F+33 (0)1 44 61 85 00
latitudes.consultants@wanadoo.fr

Bernard Ferrari
La Griaz 74310 Les Houches
T+33 (0)4 50 54 43 93
F+33 (0)4 50 54 46 01
bernard.ferrari@wanadoo.fr

Philippe Ferrer
98 rue Duguesclin 69006 Lyon
T+33 (0)4 37 43 65 33
P+33 (0)6 13 61 89 88
ferrer.p@free.fr
www.ferrerphilippe.com

Michel Freudiger
6 rue Jules Chaplain 75006 Paris France
T+33 (0)1 53 10 13 00
F+33 (0)1 53 10 13 01
michel.freudiger.architecte@wanadoo.fr

Galerie Saint Jacques
11 rue Pierre de Fermat 31000 Toulouse
T+33 (0)5 61 52 40 71
F+33 (0)5 61 52 38 99
contact@galeriesaintjacques.com
www.galeriesaintjacques.com

Frédéric Gaunet
10 rue Chevalier Saint George 75001 Paris
T+33 (0)1 42 96 86 86
info@fredericgaunet.com
www.fredericgaunet.com

GNX Architectes
215 rue Albert Sarrault 17940 Rivedoux Plage
T/F+33 (0)5 46 00 19 99
gnx.architecture@orange.fr
www.gnxarchitecture.com

Cyrille Groubé
18 rue Orfila 75020 Paris
T+33 (0)6 31 75 66 99
cyrille.groube@orange.fr

Hugues d'Hachon
2 rue Cacault 44000 Nantes
T+33 (0)2 40 48 51 67
F+33 (0)2 40 35 61 46
www.bureau-dachon.com

Idoine
72 rue Amelot 75011 Paris
T+33 (0)1 42 06 10 10
F+33 (0)1 42 06 24 30
mfaure@idoine.fr
www.groupeidoine.com

Link Agency
12 rue de la Paix 75002 Paris
T+33 (0)1 53 05 94 50
alex@linkagency.fr
www.linkagency.fr

Thierry Lombardi
54 rue Saint Suffren 13006 Marseille
T+33 (0)4 94 25 87 08
F+33 (0)4 94 05 96 14
contact@thierrylombardi.com
www.thierrylombardi.com

David Lucas
20 rue Danielle Casanova 75002 Paris
T+33 (0)1 47 03 92 04
www.davidlucas.fr
davidlucas75@hotmail.fr

Simone Micheli
Via Aretina 197r/ 199r/ 201r 50136 Firenze Italy
simone@simonemicheli.com
www.simonemicheli.com

Nahk Architecture
Christophe Dubost,
Julien Guénégou et Nicolas Rochiccioli
19 rue du Chalet 75010 Paris
T+33 (0)9 81 86 98 87
F+33 (0)9 81 70 37 44
nahk.architecture@gmail.com
http://nahk.architecture.over-blog.fr

Karl Nawrot
Zeeburgerpad 53, 1019 AB Amsterdam
The Netherlands
karlnawrot@gmail.com

Jean-Philippe Nuel
9 boulevard de la Marne 94130 Nogent-sur-Marne
T+33 (0)1 45 14 12 10
F+33 (0)1 48 77 26 92
jpn@jeanphilippenuel.com
www.jeanphilippenuel.com

Andrée Putman
83 avenue Denfert-Rochereau 75014 Paris
T+33 (0)1 55 42 88 55
F+33 (0)1 55 42 88 50
contact@andreeputman.com
www.andreeputman.com

Patrick Ribes
5 rue du Général de Castelnau 75015 Paris
T+33 (0)1 45 27 61 36
F+33 (0)1 45 27 61 82
agence@patrickribes.com
www.patrickribes.com

Jacques Rival
1 rue Duviard 69004 Lyon
T+33 (0)4 78 27 44 51
jacques@rival.fr
www.rival.fr

Joël Robinson
Parc d'activité de la Vatine
7 rue Jacques Monod 76130 Mont Saint Aignan
T+33 (0)2 35 59 20 80
F+33 (0)2 35 59 20 89
accueil@robinson-architectes.fr
www.robinson-architectes.fr

Jocelyne & Jean-Louis Sibuet
Chemin du Petit Darbon
144 Demi Quartier 74120 Megève
T+33 (0)4 50 90 63 20
contact@sibuethotels-spa.com
www.groupe-sibuet.com

Peter Stelzner
P+33 (0)6 64 35 80 93
peter@rabbitontheroof.com
www.rabbitontheroof.com

Lisbeth Strohmenger & Karen Reichenheim
63 route d'Ingwiller 67290 La Petite Pierre
T+33 (0)3 88 71 75 00
F+33 (0)3 88 70 41 05
info@laclairiere.com
www.la-clairiere.com

Pascal Thomas
7 rue principale 67290 La Petite Pierre
T+33 (0)3 88 70 45 70
T+33 (0)3 88 70 45 71
architecte.thomas@orange.fr

Trio Ingénierie / Philippe Blanc
3 place Christiane Frahier
78100 Saint-Germain-en-Laye
T+33 (0)1 39 58 37 30
F+33 (0)1 39 58 42 46
trio-ingenierie@wanadoo.fr

Luc Vaichere Architectes Associés
Les Docks de l'Untxin
9 rue Poutillenia 64122 Socoa
T+33 (0)5 59 24 97 90
F+33 (0)5 59 22 35 00
agence@lv2a.com
www.lv2a.com

Western Design
12 rue d'Enghien 75010 Paris
T+33 (0)1 53 34 18 88
F+33 (0)1 53 34 18 19
contact@westerndesign.fr
www.westerndesign.fr

Sylvie Zerat
9 rue Devès 92200 Neuilly-sur-Seine
T+33 (0)6 10 25 20 77
sz@sylvie-zerat.com
www.sylvie-zerat.com

Alexandre Zouari
1 avenue du Président Wilson 75116 Paris
T+33 (0)1 47 23 79 00
contact@alexandre-zouari.com
www.alexandre-zouari.com